PRAISE FOR
PRAYER EVANGELISM

My prayer is that every church would catch the vision detailed in this book. Imagine what would happen if all believers prayed for, cared for and shared the gospel with all their neighbors!

Neil T. Anderson

PRESIDENT, FREEDOM IN CHRIST MINISTRIES

Prayer Evangelism is a profound work of vision and biblical authority that charts the course for spiritual awakening and the transformation of our cities.

Jay Bennett

PRESIDENT, KINGDOM OIL, MINNEAPOLIS, MINNESOTA

As I was reading *Prayer Evangelism*, every spark of love for the lost came alive within me. Ed Silvoso has beautifully integrated the major components of prayer and evangelism.

Bobbye Byerly

DIRECTOR OF PRAYER AND INTERCESSION, WORLD PRAYER CENTER

Ed Silvoso again gives us the real thing: conceptual breakthroughs, dramatic anecdotes, profound spiritual insights and, above all else, the gift of faith and encouragement that, if heeded, will reenergize tired believers and change history.

John Dawson

AUTHOR OF *HEALING AMERICA'S WOUNDS* AND *TAKING OUR CITIES FOR GOD*

Ed Silvoso inspires and motivates his readers to a bold commitment in proclaiming the good news in their cities. Every single page is found gold with provocative insights and powerful Scriptural principles.

Pablo A. Deiros

PASTOR, CENTRAL BAPTIST CHURCH, BUENOS AIRES, ARGENTINA

Prayer Evangelism is an important book for twenty-first-century Christians. To win our world for Christ, we must transform our neighborhoods, schools, workplaces and homes. Ed Silvoso's prophetic message is the clearest call I have seen to help us do just that.

Dick Eastman

INTERNATIONAL PRESIDENT, EVERY HOME FOR CHRIST

This is not a book of theories but a practicioner's guide for city reaching— and more. Here is the heart of God for our communities and the means to seeing our cities healed.

Francis Frangipane

PASTOR, RIVER OF LIFE MINISTRIES, ROBINS, IOWA

Prayer Evangelism is a message of hope for all those who dream of seeing their city transformed and at the feet of Christ. I know well Ed Silvoso's heart; his passion for souls; he has written precisely what he feels and practices. Whether you are a pastor or layperson, what you will discover here will change your life and give you a new vision and enthusiasm for reaching the lost in your city.

Claudio Freidzon

PASTOR, KING OF KINGS CHURCH, BUENOS AIRES, ARGENTINA

What Michael Jordan was for basketball, what John Glenn was for space, Ed Silvoso is for the Church of this new millennium. His message is prophetic and on the leading edge, and it adds a bit of panache to an already glorious Church!

Richard Gazowsky

SENIOR PASTOR, VOICE OF PENTECOST, SAN FRANCISCO, CALIFORNIA

Ed Silvoso has long served as a general on the front lines of the battle to transform our culture for Jesus Christ through prayer and authoritative personal impact. This book provides a refreshing perspective of hope and encouragement.

Stephen Paul Goold

SENIOR PASTOR, CRYSTAL EVANGELICAL FREE CHURCH
MINNEAPOLIS, MINNESOTA

Ecclesiastical analysts observe what the Spirit *has* said to the churches. Spirit-led activists hear what the Spirit *is* saying to the churches. Ed Silvoso is a cutting-edge Spirit-led activist. We have begun to minister in our community within the biblical paradigms he describes, and God is blessing our efforts in unprecedented ways. The implementation of prayer evangelism has started a spiritual revolution in our community.

Paul E. Grabill

SENIOR PASTOR, STATE COLLEGE ASSEMBLY OF GOD
STATE COLLEGE, PENNSYLVANIA

Ed Silvoso is a gracious encourager, an effective writer and a dynamic instrument of God, awakening us to new dimensions of prayer power and evangelistic penetration.

Jack W. Hayford

CHANCELLOR, THE KING'S COLLEGE AND SEMINARY

This book will be used by thousands as the inspiration and blueprint to reach millions. Ed Silvoso shows that city reaching has been done, can be done and should be done. His methods are biblical, proven and incredibly simple!

Steve Heinz

EXECUTIVE PRODUCER, LIGHT THE NATION

Ed Silvoso's descriptions of the paradigm shifts taking place in the Church today will inspire anyone hoping to see people renewed, the marketplace reached and cities transformed for Jesus Christ.

John Isaacs

PASTOR, SOUTH BAY COVENANT CHURCH, CAMPBELL, CALIFORNIA

We have all been looking for answers on how to reach our cities for Christ. The book you hold in your hand contains the keys for successful city transformation. I got excited just reading Ed Silvoso's powerful message for this hour!

Cindy Jacobs

COFOUNDER, GENERALS OF INTERCESSION

You will be captivated by this message and compelled by the Holy Spirit to actively participate and to fulfill your destiny as a minister of the life of Christ.

Beverly Jaime

ASSOCIATE PASTOR, CATHEDRAL OF FAITH, SAN JOSE, CALIFORNIA

Ed Silvoso has taken present-day truth and revelation and combined it with prophetic insights and a pragmatic knowledge born of his experience in city reaching to give us a new paradigm of what we must do to gather the end-time harvest. This is a great book.

John P. Kelley

EXECUTIVE DIRECTOR, INTERNATIONAL COALITION OF APOSTLES

The principles contained in this book have been tested and proven effective in Singapore, where Ed Silvoso's teachings have led us to major breakthroughs in changing the old mind-sets of the Church and altering the spiritual climate over our nation.

Lawrence Khong

SENIOR PASTOR, FAITH COMMUNITY BAPTIST CHURCH, SINGAPORE

Ed Silvoso has written a practical handbook for reclaiming our cities by changing the spiritual climate over them one house at a time.

David Kiteley

SENIOR PASTOR, SHILOH CHRISTIAN FELLOWSHIP, OAKLAND, CALIFORNIA

With a passionate heart for the lost, Ed Silvoso is one of the true innovators in the Church when it comes to reaching the unsaved with the gospel. *Prayer Evangelism* is an exciting book spelling out a dynamic strategy for reaching entire cities for Christ.

Bill McCartney

FOUNDER AND PRESIDENT, PROMISE KEEPERS

This strategic book will be a practical and valuable tool in the hands of everyone who wants to help bring forth the will of God on Earth.

Terry Moore

SENIOR PASTOR, SOJOURN CHURCH, CARROLLTON, TEXAS

Encouraging! Inspiring! Equipping! As a practicioner of city reaching, I recommend *Prayer Evangelism* as the vision for the way forward. We can do this!

Jim Munson

PASTOR, CHRIST CHURCH AND CITY REACHING, APPLE VALLEY, MINNESOTA

Tested and tried in the crucible of on-site city-reaching efforts, the principles and paradigm shifts in this book are practical, powerful and Spirit-filled. As you read *Prayer Evangelism*, you will find yourself saying, "Yes, it can be done! God wants to do it, and I don't want to miss it. Our city will be reached for Jesus Christ!" Thank you, Ed Silvoso, for imparting God-empowered, city-sized faith in the hearts of future city reachers.

Dan Nold

PASTOR, CHURCH OF STATE COLLEGE, STATE COLLEGE, PENNSYLVANIA

In this increasingly post-Christian culture, we must rediscover compassion for the lost and undertake a ministry people can feel and experience. *Prayer Evangelism* realigns us with the principles of ancient biblical Christianity that will make us surprisingly relevant to the times in which we live.

Tom Pelton

PRESIDENT, MARCH FOR JESUS/JESUS DAY

The prophetic acts of a praying congregation can and will transform the spiritual atmosphere over our cities. Prodigals will return, crime rates will lower, and the coming Harvest will be released! This book shows the way. Ed Silvoso writes effectively on returning to the powerful practices of the "untrained and uneducated" saints of the Early Church, encouraging us to follow the example of those who had been with Jesus and who obeyed His command to love their neighbors as themselves.

Chuck D. Pierce

VICE-PRESIDENT, GLOBAL HARVEST MINISTRIES

Ed Silvoso cuts right through the clutter and religious verbiage of the day to give us a practical and inspiring strategy for winning the heart of a city for Christ. Numerous books have been written on how to take a city for God, but *Prayer Evangelism* stands out in the crowd. The compassion and wisdom in this book are straight from the heart of God.

Ted Roberts

SENIOR PASTOR, EAST HILL CHURCH, GRESHAM, OREGON

Dare to expose yourself to this book and old barriers to evangelism will be demolished! You will find a new freedom and enthusiasm to reach cities for Christ. *Prayer Evangelism* contains a set of blueprints that can dramatically expedite world evangelization. Since my childhood, I have known Ed Silvoso. No other Christian leader has had more influence in my life.

Sergio Scataglini

AUTHOR OF *THE FIRE OF HIS HOLINESS*

No one has made a greater impact on the Body of Christ in Silicon Valley than Ed Silvoso. It's not unusual to hear the principles he espouses on the lips of believers who don't even know his name—principles like "one church, many congregations." The movement of prayer around the San Francisco Bay Area can be directly traced to his encouragement. Live the principles in this book, and both your life and the world around you will never be the same.

David A. Seeba

CPA, HANUSH & SEEBA, INC., SAN JOSE, CALIFORNIA

Ed Silvoso has the passion of one who knows God and His love for people, cities and nations. He writes with the intensity of an evangelist who has seen the impossible made possible.

Jean Steffenson

PRESIDENT, NATIVE AMERICAN RESOURCE NETWORK

Ed Silvoso skillfully and with prophetic clarity and precision helps us to identify the shifting paradigms that will enable us to unify as a Church and to reach our communities.

J. Doug Stringer

FOUNDER, SOMEBODY CARES/TURNING POINT INTERNATIONAL

Silvoso has once again stirred my spiritual emotions as I ventured with him through this book. This timely book is going to be a textbook in my continual efforts to reach out to the First Nations of America and Canada. In his last book, *That None Should Perish*, it affected over 120 Native American tribes with a new energy of evangelism. What this new book will do for Native America, I predict will reach national media attention.

Jay Swallow

COFOUNDER, TWO RIVERS NATIVE AMERICAN TRAINING CENTER

This book is a trumpet sounding in the ear of a sleeping Church! With alarm-clock persistence, Ed Silvoso challenges us to change our mind-sets, so we can change our city. His words will disturb your peace and discomfort your nights as you come to realize that everyone you know should hear the gospel, and yet they have not.

Tommy Tenney

AUTHOR OF *THE GOD CHASERS* AND *GOD'S DREAM TEAM*

PRAYER
EVANGELISM

ED SILVOSO

Regal

A Division of Gospel Light
Ventura, California, U.S.A.

Published by Regal Books
A Division of Gospel Light
Ventura, California, U.S.A.
Printed in the U.S.A.

Cover Design by Robert Williams
Interior Design by Robert Williams
Edited by David Webb and Wil Simon

Library of Congress Cataloging-in-Publication Data
Silvoso, Ed.
    Prayer evangelism / Ed Silvoso.
        p.   cm.
    Includes bibliographical references.
    ISBN 0-8307-2397-8
    1. Evangelistic work.   2. Prayer—Christianity.   3. Cities and towns—Religious aspects—Christianity.   I. Title.

    BV3793 .S467   2000
    269'.2—dc21   00-055281

8   9   10   11   12   13   14   15   /   13   12   11   10   09

Rights for publishing this book in other languages are contracted by Gospel Literature International (GLINT). GLINT also provides technical help for the adaptation, translation and publishing of Bible study resources and books in scores of languages worldwide. For further information, write to GLINT, P.O. Box 4060, Ontario, CA 91761-1003, U.S.A. You may also send e-mail to Glintint@aol.com, or visit the GLINT website at www.glint.org.

To Dave and Sue Thompson,

lifelong friends and faithful partners

in reaching cities for Christ.

CONTENTS

FOREWORD

Ed Silvoso is one of the great evangelical visionaries and strategists of our time. The zeal and energy he expends in the spreading of the gospel are boundless and inspiring. A fount of evangelistic wisdom from the Holy Spirit, Ed will not be satisfied until every city and every person on the planet are won for Christ—or until our Lord returns. He will work feverishly until that day, and so should we. The Lord raised up Ed Silvoso for this hour, the most profound window of time in all of history. Advances in technology and high-speed worldwide transportation have provided us with new tools for tackling the Great Commission, the fulfillment of which is within reach.

In the last century, the world population exploded. Until about 1850, the world population was less than 1 billion. By about 1930, it had doubled to 2 billion. By 1974, the world population had doubled again to 4 billion. The population recently surpassed 6 billion and at this rate will double again in less than 20 years. Our cities are burgeoning with growth. The fields are white unto harvest. This is God's hour.

Through Campus Crusade for Christ and our partnership activities, we saw 1.223 billion exposures to the gospel in 1999, with 24.1 million people indicating salvation decisions for Christ. And this was only among live audiences and does not include exposure through our radio or television programs. *The World Almanac* estimates that in A.D. 1 the entire population of the world was only 200 million! As of January 2000, Campus Crusade had 21,952 staff members and 488,917 trained volunteers working in 186 countries representing 99.84 percent of the world's population. Our *Jesus* film has been translated into 582 languages and has been seen by 3.1 billion people in 228 countries.

I say all that to make a point: The Holy Spirit is reaching all over this world to bring people the most joyful news ever announced. Yet multitudes in our own cities have never heard a clear presentation of the gospel—who Jesus is and how His great love and mercy were demonstrated in His atonement.

Our cities, our Jerusalems, are Ed's burden, and God has given him creative insights into how to win our cities for Christ through prayer evangelism. There has never been a more urgent or opportune time to share the gospel. We must act, and we must act now. We will not pass this way again.

May the Lord use this book to inspire, motivate and help equip every reader to help take his or her city for Christ.

Bill Bright

FOUNDER AND PRESIDENT
CAMPUS CRUSADE FOR CHRIST INTERNATIONAL

Go Tell It on the Plaza

Nothing is more extraordinary than being born again—that instant when we turned from darkness to light and saw Jesus with His arms extended towards us. We all remember the moment when we crossed the threshold from death to life, when we learned that our names had been written in the book of life by God Himself. All other events in life pale in comparison.

Once we have experienced this rebirth, we want everybody else to have the same experience. We want to see our loved ones come to Jesus. We want strangers who live in foreign lands to know Him. The Holy Spirit of God who now dwells within us has put this desire in our hearts.

Paradoxically, most of us are paralyzed by the mere thought of witnessing to others, especially strangers. We *want* to tell them about Jesus so that they will experience the miracle of the new birth; but when we go to speak, our lips seemed to be glued together and our voices desert us at the crucial moment. We have tried and failed so many times that we feel as though we will never be able to do it.

This realization pains us deeply because Jesus told us to do it and we *do* want to please Him. Worse, we are tortured by the two-edged pain of letting Him down and the certainty that people within our circle of influence are going to hell.

This book has been written in part to help you overcome this fear and pain. The ideas and strategies contained in these pages are drawn from lessons I learned in my own struggle with shyness and my deep-seated fear of talking to strangers. I write not as a theologian, which I am not, but as a practitioner deeply committed to the Scriptures and to the fulfillment of the Great Commission.

More importantly, this book is based on the victories of thousands of men and women I have met in cities all over the world—people like myself who not long ago were afraid of telling others about Jesus and today are telling entire cities about Him! These once-shy warriors today are seeing relatives, friends and associates turn from darkness to life, from the dominion of Satan to the kingdom of God. And they are enjoying it!

It is my hope and my prayer that you will be liberated and empowered by the biblical principles taught in this book and that you will go beyond merely witnessing to the people near to you. I pray you will see *your entire city reached for Christ*. As you read this book, you will see that it can be done. Better yet, it *will* be done!

1

WHAT THE DEVIL DOESN'T WANT YOU TO KNOW

You may be down, but Satan is down, too. The one who gets up first will win your city.

If you are a city reacher, you are likely no stranger to discouragement. Many in this area of ministry have experienced its force at high tide. You probably have felt, if only for a fleeting moment, the stinging doubts that mercilessly shout at you that you have chased an impossible dream, an unrealistic vision. You have been down, and you may be afraid that you are down for the full count. If this is your situation, then I have good news: There is hope.

I have been involved in city-reaching efforts since 1990, when our ministry, Harvest Evangelism, facilitated the first such thrust in the city of Resistencia, Argentina. Our efforts were successful and, in 1994, Regal Books published *That None Should*

Perish, in which I described the biblical principles behind Plan Resistencia. In that book, I also introduced prayer evangelism as a potent vehicle for reaching cities.

Soon we found ourselves involved in more than a hundred cities on five continents, facilitating city-reaching thrusts á la Resistencia. Things could not have gone better. People were being saved, lives were being changed, and entire cities were undergoing transformation.

Nevertheless, by March 1999 we had become overwhelmed by tremendous challenges, almost to the point of despair. Our team had pioneered new concepts, conquered new territory and facilitated unprecedented breakthroughs in cities around the world; but the intensity of those efforts had taken their toll and had exposed us to spiritual attacks, and I was feeling the pain.

In a moment of unhealthy self-pity I began to tell the Lord how badly wounded I was, how much our family and our team had suffered, how brutal the blows had been and how little return we had seen on our investment. The Lord's reply shocked me: *Ed, you should see the* other *guy!* He *is the one who looks really bad. You're on the winning team! If you think you look pathetic, just imagine how awful the loser must look.*

Just then, a scene from the movie *Rocky II* came to my mind. It happens toward the end of the climactic title fight. Rocky Balboa and Apollo Creed have slugged it out to the point of total exhaustion. Both of them are down, lying on the canvas, and the referee has begun the count. Rocky's manager, crusty old Mickey, is frantically shouting in Rocky's dull ears, "Get up, you bum. Get uuuup!" He keeps on screaming until Rocky, in obvious pain and with great difficulty, begins to pull himself up while the count continues. Under Mickey's unrelenting verbal shoving, Rocky keeps riding waves of exhaustion on a raging sea of suffering. And when the referee cries, "...9...10. You're out!" Rocky is the one standing over the downed Apollo. Our hero stands for only a few moments, but he is on his feet long enough to be declared the winner and new champion.

As I reflected on this dramatic scene, I sensed the Lord saying to me, *Get up and claim the prize! You are down* but so is the devil. *He does not want you to know it, but he is totally spent after such a fight. He has no more strength, and this is why he is so bent on keeping you focused on your own wounds. Both of you are down; but the one who gets up and claims the prize wins. Get up, you blessed one!*

This experience enabled me to understand a powerful dynamic concerning trials: Trials require two fiercely opposing parties for its painful pressure to develop. Pressure, like a pincer, needs two anchor points to operate. We are one of the points; the devil is the other one. However, in the midst of these frays, we tend to focus exclusively on the damage done to us or to our loved ones. We seldom, if ever, realize what the trial has done to the opposition. Consider the way most Christians process Job's tribulation. We concentrate almost exclusively on what Job lost and how much he suffered, and we fail to see the main point in this epic drama: *The devil lost big to a mere human being.* Satan ended up discredited and humiliated before his own demons. What the devil values the most, his pride, lay shattered at Job's feet.

Take heart that even though we suffer, we *always* end up stronger than the devil. This is also true with regard to where we find ourselves today in the city-reaching movement after a decade of intense struggle. We have made tremendous strides, and unprecedented breakthroughs have in fact taken place. True, progress has come at a cost. And Satan wants us to focus on our cost so that we will not see what *his* cost has been! He knows that if we are discouraged and preoccupied with our wounds, we will fail to understand just how close we are to seeing the greatest outpouring ever of God's Spirit on the cities of this world. The devil's scheme is to keep us focused on *our* pain rather than his.

The Prize Is Within Reach

Why do we struggle so against the devil? Because he is the one blinding the lost to the truth of the gospel.

> The god of this world has blinded the minds of the unbelieving, that they might not see the light of the gospel of the glory of Christ (2 Cor. 4:4).

Yes, we struggle with the enemy in other areas, but none of these is as significant. Satan cannot snatch us away from the Savior's hand, so our salvation is secure (see John 10:28). What the devil intends for evil, God uses for good, so the outcome of our trials and tribulations is bound to be positive (see Gen. 50:20; Rom. 8:28). Even in the areas where we have willfully sinned, the Holy Spirit is actively at work, bringing us to repentance; and when we repent, the blood of Jesus graciously erases the marks of sin (see 1 Pet. 1:2).

On none of those fronts—salvation, tribulations and sanctification—can the devil harm the followers of Christ. So the primary purpose of our struggles against the devil is to open the eyes of the lost to the gospel:

> I am sending you to them to open their eyes and turn them from darkness to light, and from the power of Satan to God (Acts 26:17,18, *NIV*).

This is the *only* struggle where the devil has a fighting chance. So when I refer to the devil in this book, it will usually be in the context of his opposition to the fulfillment of the Great Commission. I do not believe there is a demon hiding behind every bush or hanging out on every street corner, but I do believe the Bible teaches that there are forces of wickedness and powers who rule over the darkness in our cities. Such are the strongholds we will address here, for this is a struggle that requires us to employ a powerful tool like prayer evangelism.

A decade has now passed since we began to teach and apply the principles of prayer evangelism to city-reaching efforts. During that time we have seen a few cities reached for Christ and their spiritual climate changed, at least for a season. We have also seen scores of cities begin to undergo the same process. This is excellent news. But we have not yet seen a steady stream of cities transformed, and this realization hurts. When the devil taunts us with statistics, usually in our moments of vulnerability, we are tempted to jump into the pool of self-pity. If this is where you are at, if your city has not been reached for Christ, don't jump! There *is* hope and plenty of it, as you will read in this book.

Powerful changes are taking place in the Church and in our cities—changes beyond anything imaginable only a few years ago. These are not superficial changes but changes in *paradigms*. When considered one by one, the changes may not seem impressive; but when viewed as pieces of a puzzle that is fast coming together, the revolutionary implications come into clear focus: *The Church can change the spiritual climate over the city.* This rediscovery of biblical principles for reaching entire regions can ignite city-reaching thrusts, moving them forward and upward in exciting new ways. And as we learn how to transform the spiritual atmosphere over a region, the uplifting, cozy climate that characterizes many pastors' prayer summits and intercessory gatherings can be spread throughout our cities.

The transformation of cities is no longer a distant hope but, rather, it is a fast-approaching reality that can be yours once you grasp and activate the biblical principles involved. The heart of this hope lies in a series of paradigm shifts that have begun to take place in the Church in recent years—and a few others that are about to.

A paradigm is a conceptual grid through which reality is perceived. A *paradigm shift* is a change in that grid that enables us to see reality in a different, often more effective way. Paradigm shifts are the hinges upon which the door to discoveries and scientific breakthroughs is opened. For example, mankind had tried to achieve flight for thousands of years with no success. Our ancestors explored every imaginable way to make the human body fly like the birds of the air. Leonardo da Vinci even glued feathers to his body and, while perched on the banister of a second floor balcony, vigorously flapped his arms in a failed attempt to take off. Nothing worked until Wilbur and Orville Wright had a paradigm shift: They discovered that the key to flying lies in the *shape* of the wing. The Wright brothers found that wind rushing over a wing with a flat bottom and a curved top creates the physical dynamics required to lift a vehicle off the ground.[1] Once the Wright brothers perceived reality in a different way, people began to fly, and the impossible became possible.

A paradigm shift also represents a transition in thinking that is irreversible. Like a cracking in the ice on a lake at the beginning of spring—once it happens, however miniscule the crack, the ice never will recover its old form but will continue cracking and breaking until the ice takes on a whole new form (water). This is why the paradigm shifts I describe in this book are so significant. The Church, already being affected by them, will never be the same. Granted, some of the new paradigms are not yet fully visible, as they are in their beginning stages; but like that first crack in the ice, they are irreversible and will only grow larger.

In the chapters that follow, I will identify and define 17 different paradigm shifts—some that have already begun to alter the landscape of the Church and our cities, others that are on the horizon. At one time or another, most of these paradigms have been embraced or espoused by individuals in the Church. What is new today, however, is that these paradigms are fast becoming part of the Church's life stream and are quietly changing its course. What I am describing is something like the onset of puberty. When our brains released hormones for the first time into our puerile bloodstreams, we did not know, much less understand, what was going on; but we were changed nonetheless. Voice, hair, skin, emotions, the way we related to the opposite sex—everything changed drastically. Something similar is happening to the Church today.

The Church that is arising as a result of the new paradigms is stronger, healthier, mightier and more than capable of transforming our cities for Christ by changing their spiritual climate. That is

THE CHURCH THAT IS ARISING IS STRONGER, HEALTHIER, MIGHTIER AND CAPABLE OF TRANSFORMING OUR CITIES FOR CHRIST BY CHANGING THEIR SPIRITUAL CLIMATE.

what this book is all about. I fervently pray that as you read, you will be encouraged, strengthened and equipped for taking the gospel to your neighborhood, your city, your nation and beyond.

Like Rocky's manager, I say to you, "Get up, you blessed soldier! Get up! You may be down, but Satan is down, too, and the
one who gets up first wins cities. Get up and claim the prize.
Your city is waiting to be reached!"

Paradigm Shifts and Prophetic Acts

Prophetic acts are found all through the Bible. God told
Jeremiah to go to the potter's house to watch a vessel be broken
and re-formed as an object lesson of how God changes the
natural through the supernatural (see Jer. 18:1-10). In another
instance, a stone was tied to a book of prophecies and cast into
the Euphrates River to illustrate God's upcoming judgment
against Babylon (see Jer. 51:60-64).

The institution of the Lord's Supper was also a prophetic
act. Jesus broke the bread and blessed the cup to symbolize not
only His upcoming death but also the redemption that would
flow out of it. In the natural, betrayal (by Judas), abandonment
(by the disciples) and forsakenness (by God) were prevailing factors in Christ's death on the cross. Through this prophetic act,
however, Jesus built a bridge of faith into a new reality of redemption and reconciliation. Prophetic acts are important and
powerful agents of change.

Usually a paradigm shift, in its early stages, insinuates
itself through a prophetic act. And to fully understand paradigm shifts, we need to understand their beginnings in
prophetic acts. A prophetic act is the modeling in microcosm
of a truth that is not evident in the corresponding macrocosm.
It is a living parable in which the performers embrace and
represent truth that is being denied or opposed in the larger
context. For instance, when a group of white pastors humbly

wash the feet of nonwhite pastors and beg their forgiveness for the horrible sin of racism, such action constitutes a prophetic act. This gesture in and of itself is too small to heal the scourge of racism; but it is a representative act that is powerful enough to launch or aid the healing process that eventually will eradicate racism.

We are instructed not to despise small beginnings (see Zech. 4:10). Small beginnings, like the tiny stream that eventually joins others to form the mighty Amazon River in South America, have the built-in potential to expand exponentially. A paradigm shift, though small at first when introduced through a prophetic act, is *never* irrelevant. There is no telling how much an almost imperceptible shift in paradigms can change everything around us. This is what happened in my hometown in 1997.

I was born and raised in the city of San Nicolas, Argentina. As a teenager, I sat by the bank of the Parana River on Thursday evenings to talk to God about revival. During the 1960s and 1970s my city became a spiritual beacon of hope as the Church and its many congregations grew and infiltrated the city's social strata with the light of the gospel. Scores of lives were changed. New church buildings sprang up in barrios. A new batch of pastors joined the old ones to care for increasing numbers of new converts—until something happened that was intriguing at first but catastrophic in the end!

A spiritual entity disguised as Mary, the earthly mother of our Savior, "appeared" to a simple local woman. The apparition known as the Queen of Heaven took the form of the weeping virgin, as tears showed up on the marble face of a statue of Mary. Pilgrims began to flock to San Nicolas in huge numbers, and soon a shrine was built. Unfortunately, as this new cult flourished, the city wilted. Major industries shut down. Commerce came to a standstill. Crime increased beyond the power of the police to control it. Nasty church splits took place. Pastors died prematurely, pastoral oversight of the city became nonexistent, and the spiritual climate turned hostile. Our shining city on a hill, spiritually speaking, crumbled into a valley of despair, and a spiritual oasis turned into a wilderness.

However, all of that began to change through a prophetic act on July 21, 1997. Our team from Harvest Evangelism, along with 360 delegates from four continents, joined the pastors and elders of the Church in San Nicolas at the seven gates of the city to perform a three-part prophetic act.

First, we repented publicly for sin inside the Church that had allowed catastrophic sin to come into the city. Dr. Charles H. Kraft writes that demons are like rats who have infested a house because they are drawn to the spiritual garbage inside. If you have a problem with rats, don't blame the rats. It is your garbage. Clean up your garbage, and the rats will go someplace else.[2] The pastors of San Nicolas took full responsibility, because they now understood that every major problem in the city (macrocosm) is *always* a magnified expression of unresolved problems in the Church (microcosm). Darkness can only prosper in the absence of light.

Secondly, we declared in united prayer at the gates of the city that the city of San Nicolas belonged to God. The pastors then drove into the ground stakes inscribed with Bible promises at each one of the gates. They took turns with the hammer, and each blow was accompanied by a prophetic utterance. Declarations such as "San Nicolas is a city of victory and not of defeat" and "Jesus is the Lord of the city, not the Queen of Heaven" were spoken out loud and in faith.

Thirdly, a proclamation was read, stating that San Nicolas belongs to the Lord, who bought the city with His blood and who keeps it by His grace. The proclamation was broadcast all over the city on radio.

This exercise was followed by united church services the next day and by three evening radio broadcasts, Monday through Wednesday. The broadcasts were hosted by pastors representing the denominational composition of the Church in the city. These broadcasts enabled believers all over town to do three things: (1) to dedicate their homes as lighthouses of prayer on Monday; (2) to spiritually cleanse their homes on Tuesday; and (3) to prayer walk their neighborhoods on Wednesday. By the end of the three-day event, there were lighthouses of prayer in every neighborhood, and the entire city had been prayed over. Many found the Lord at a prayer fair held the following Saturday, and the week climaxed with a powerful and moving united Communion service the next day.

The results? That week the crime rate in the city dropped dramatically. In fact, not a single major crime was reported. Pastors who had been a party to divisions repented publicly and made restitution to those they had wronged. The media opened their doors to the Church. Public offi-cials asked for personal prayer and for prayer meetings to be held in govern-ment buildings. Best of all, prodigals returned to Christ, and unbelievers were asking to be led to the Lord. *In just one week, the spiritual climate over the city had changed dramatically.*

But that was not the end of it. Many of the 360 visiting delegates went back to their home countries on five conti-nents and performed similar prophetic acts with similar results. Today, scores of cities have experienced a change for the better in their spiritual climates as an

PROPHETIC ACTS ARE POWERFUL BECAUSE THEY EXPRESS ON EARTH WHAT GOD HAS ALREADY DECREED IN HEAVEN.

indirect result of what was done in San Nicolas—an impressive harvest whose genesis was the unpretentious seed first planted in my hometown. On October 16, 1999, from Madison Square Garden in New York, we broadcast to 572 television downlink sites in 50 states to facilitate all over the United States what was pioneered by the pastors in San Nicolas.

At the time of these events, we did not see clearly the implications of our prophetic acts; but now, with the perspective of time, we are able to better grasp why so much happened in such a short time in San Nicolas and why these wonderful things continue to happen all over the world. Shifts in paradigms made them inevitable. The prophetic acts of the pastors in San Nicolas were powerful, not in and of themselves, but because they provided a conduit to express on Earth what God had already decreed in heaven.

The Power of Prophetic Acts

Why are prophetic acts so powerful? When I inquired of the Lord, He directed me to John 8:44, where Jesus speaks to the Pharisees, saying:

> You are of your father the devil, and you want to do the desires of your father. He was a murderer from the beginning, and does not stand in the truth, because there is no truth in him. Whenever he speaks a lie, he speaks from his own nature; for he is a liar, and the father of lies.

The context here is one of religious unbelief. Jesus is speaking to religious leaders who stubbornly refuse to accept the truth He preaches. His statement that the devil cannot stand in the truth because there is no truth in him contains the key to understanding the power of prophetic acts.

When we read that the devil is a liar, we assume that he lies to us but not to his minions. If the devil were to speak the truth to his demons, he would have to disclose certain unpleasant facts about the end of time—facts concerning the lake of fire, their eternal demise and Satan's utter defeat. If he were to let them in on news of their fate, it is safe to assume that his troops would not fight for him so intensely.

The primary intent of a lie is always to exert some form of control over the person being lied to. The truth is always more powerful than lies; but those who believe a lie come, within the scope of the lie, under the control of the liar. In the case of the Pharisees, the words of Jesus failed to register with them because they had accepted a lie instead. For centuries the devil has told the same lies: "White Christians will never repent and make restitution to the nonwhite people they have wronged through the ages. Gentiles will never love Jews. Men will never honor and respect women but will only wish to exploit them." Such ludicrous statements become more believable when they are sustained by hatred that is validated by human self-centeredness. This was the case in America where, at one time, the Supreme Court ruled that blacks were not equal to whites in the eyes of the law; and in Europe, where the Church did not denounce or oppose murderous ethnic cleansings. In such cases the lies of the devil become incorporated into the cultural fiber of a nation.

On the other hand, when even a small group, made up of people affected by such lies, performs a prophetic act that exemplifies and declares the opposite of what a particular lie proclaims, then a circle of truth is painted around the devil, thereby exposing his scheme for all to see, for he cannot stand in the truth.

To be successful, a liar must conceal the fact that he is a liar; otherwise no one will believe his lies. The devil avoids truth so his cover will not be blown. A prophetic act does exactly that, altering and eventually exposing, through the insertion of truth, the devil's carefully orchestrated cover of intertwined lies.

Our hour of opportunity comes once a lie is exposed and its aura of immutability removed. Although circumstances in the natural realm may still look the same, a prophetic act calls the things that are not as though they are. In an act of spiritual warfare directed at the devil, we confess with our lips what we have chosen to believe in our hearts. This is clearly implied in Revelation 12:11, where we are told that the devil is defeated by the blood of the Lamb, the word of our testimony (confession) and a commitment to warfare so fierce that we despise our lives even unto death.

Spiritual truth can never remain dormant; it has to be declared. And when it is, the truth challenges and eventually changes that which opposes it. As a result, what was thought to be impossible (through Satan's lie) now becomes possible (through Jesus' truth)—not just in that time and place but beyond. Like ripples in a pond, the spoken truth moves outward in ever-expanding circles set into motion by the initial prophetic act.

When we punch a hole in the darkness, at first light just filters in through the hole. But the light keeps on spreading, until the once-impenetrable mantle of blackness eventually dissipates. This is why such a simple but courageous act not only destroyed the absoluteness of Satan's deception in San Nicolas—that the city was his and nothing would ever change the spiritual status quo—but also continues to spread hope around the world.

The paradigm shifts we will look at in this book usually came into focus first as prophetic acts. Small, isolated and apparently insignificant though not irrelevant, these acts birthed something that continues to expand and grow. What were in the beginning small streams in remote areas of the jungle are gradually coming together to forge mighty rivers. Come with me as we explore these streams and river to determine what has happened so far, how much more is and will be happening and how close we are to claiming the prize.

But first, we must equip ourselves with a very important tool that makes the journey possible: prayer evangelism.

Note
1. NASA, "What Makes An Airplane Fly—Level 1," *ALLSTAR (Aeronautics Learning Laboratory for Science, Technology and Research) Network*, February 29, 2000. http://www.allstar.fiu.edu/aero/fltmidfly.htm (accessed June 7, 2000). Lift is that force which opposes the force of gravity (or weight). Lift is produced by a lower pressure created on the upper surface of an airplane's wing compared to the pressure on the wing's lower surface, causing the wing to be lifted upward. The special shape of the airplane wing, called an airfoil, is designed so that air flowing over the wing will have to travel a greater distance faster, resulting in a lower pressure area and thus lifting the wing upward.
2. Charles H. Kraft, "In Dark Dungeons of Collective Captivity: Response," in *Wrestling with Dark Angels*, ed. C. Peter Wagner and F. Douglas Pennoyer, (Ventura, CA: Regal Books, 1990), p. 276.

2

Prayer Evangelism According to Jesus

Before we can change the spiritual climate over our cities, we must have a working knowledge of one of our primary tools: prayer evangelism. I introduced the concept of prayer evangelism in *That None Should Perish* in 1994, but since then much has been learned from using this potent weapon on the front lines. Several years of working side by side with pastors and leaders in cities all over the world have enriched tremendously our initial understanding of this concept.

Simply put, prayer evangelism is talking to God about our neighbors before we talk to our neighbors about God. This definition, coined by Beverly Jaime,[1] has helped us to put at ease thousands of Christians who have a genuine desire to witness to the lost but who feel inadequate or scared to share the gospel with them.

I know those feelings of inadequacy very well; they used to torment me as a brand-new Christian. Shortly after my conversion, a visiting evangelist pounded on the pulpit at my church and declared, "No one should hear the gospel twice until everybody has heard it once! Therefore, since all of you have heard it more than once, I will not preach to you. Instead, I will organize you into pairs to witness door-to-door to those who have not heard it yet." At that moment panic struck, and I found myself foolishly wishing that an earthquake, a tornado, a flood, *anything* catastrophic, would hit our town so I would not have to go out to witness to strangers.

Why such a negative reaction? I wasn't opposed to witnessing; I was just scared of talking to strangers. Being the shy person that I was, even if I had mustered enough courage to *try*, fear of rejection would probably have immobilized me anyway.

As it turned out, neither flood nor earthquake hit town to alleviate my anxiety. So I began to fervently hope I would be paired with a vivacious, engaging, talkative individual—someone to whom I could say, "Obviously, you have the gift and the anointing for door-to-door evangelism. You take the point and talk to people, while I step into the background and silently pray for you." But it was not to happen that way.

Although I was painfully shy, I had always been perceived by my peers to be a leader—a shy leader but a leader nonetheless. As far back as I can remember, I was expected to lead. So, under the watchful gaze of the fiery evangelist, my pastor told me, "Ed, we are going to team you up with a younger Christian so you can show him how to do it." Me? Show someone else how to do it? I did not know how to witness myself! But soon I found myself and my young charge walking up to a door that, to me, resembled the entrance to a lion's den.

Under the admiring gaze of my pupil, I knocked on the door as softly as I could, fervently hoping that no one would be home. I heard steps approaching, and I dearly wished it would be a child, no more than 3 or 4 years old, so I could sit down with him and just talk for the next hour while others from my church visited the rest of the block.

I was so ashamed of my cowardliness! Fear and shame are a lethal combination for an aspiring evangelist. Even though I wanted to do great things for God, I was threatened by the prospect of having to share the gospel with total strangers.

However, all that changed the day I discovered the dynamic, biblical principle of prayer evangelism.

Prayer Evangelism in Four Easy Steps

Whatever house you enter, first say, "Peace be to this house." And whatever city you enter, and they receive you, eat what is set before you; and heal those in it who are sick, and say to them, "The kingdom of God has come near to you" (Luke 10:5,8,9).

The principles of prayer evangelism are taught in several places in the Bible, but the most complete model is found in this passage. This is the only occasion in the Gospels where Jesus spells out an evangelistic method. Here He calls for us to do four things for the lost:

1. Speak peace to them.
2. Fellowship with them.
3. Take care of their needs.
4. Proclaim the good news.

The first of these four steps will open the door to the second step and so forth. It is very important for us to understand that the steps are interconnected and, to be effective, must be implemented in the order given. We will soon see why this is so.

This four-step method proved so successful that soon after Jesus taught it to His disciples, multitudes came to believe in Jesus and demons surrendered en masse to a bunch of rookie evangelists. Unfortunately, these are not the results we see today when we evangelize. What is the problem? Rather than following Jesus' four-step approach, we reverse the order and begin with the last step, witnessing, and skip the blessing, the fellowship and the caring that are to precede the good news. In most cases, this approach to witnessing does not work.

We knock on a door—many times out of guilt or, as in my case, pressure—and if that door opens a crack, we get three minutes of reluctant attention. And two and a half of those minutes are wasted explaining the difference between us and the Jehovah's Witnesses!

Why should the people in that house believe that we—complete strangers—are going to heaven and that they are going to hell? Why should they believe that the Bible is the Word of God? To them, the Bible is no different than the book of Mormon or the sayings of Buddha or Mao. What credibility do we have to cause them to believe anything we say? For credibility to develop, a process is necessary. This is where prayer evangelism comes in.

The beginning of Jesus' prescribed process calls for us to become shepherds to the people in our circle of influence. They may not yet know that we are their pastors; but we should know they are our sheep. We must begin by caring for them. This attitude is at the heart of Jesus' strategy.

We Must Make Peace with the Lost

Jesus' method of evangelism calls for us to first speak peace over the lost. This is important for at least three reasons.

Reason #1: We need to declare peace because we, as Christians, have been at war with the lost. Too often, "Repent or burn" is the banner under which we approach the unsaved of this world. Unfortunately, we have a tendency to strongly dislike sinners, and this soon becomes obvious to them. Our bellicose attitudes do tremendous disservice to Jesus, who in His earthly days was glad to be known as a friend of sinners. If Jesus is their friend, we cannot be their enemies.

I became aware of my own belligerence toward the lost the first time I tried to implement the Luke 10 strategy in our neighborhood. Instead of claiming the promises of God to deal with the problems I saw in my neighbors' lives, I told God about everything that was wrong with these people. I talked to Him in disgust about the unwed mother and how she *had* to change because she was such a bad example to my daughters. I demanded that He do something about the couple who kept us awake at night with their arguing and fighting. I complained about the depressive neighbor whose front yard was a disgrace and a bane to real estate values on our block. And of course I did not forget about the teenager on drugs. I made it perfectly clear to the Lord what a detriment this young man was to our neighborhood.

All of a sudden, I sensed God saying, "Ed, I am so glad you have not witnessed to any of these yet."

Surprised, I asked, "Lord, why is that?"

His reply was very sobering: "Because I don't want your neighbors to know that you and I are related. I hurt when they hurt. I reach out to them. I constantly extend grace to them. I am the God who causes the sun to rise over the righteous and unrighteous alike. I love them. But you don't. You resent them.

Rather than being an advocate for them, a lawyer for the defense, you are instead a witness for the prosecution . . . if not the prosecutor himself." Then He rebuked me, saying, "Ed, unless you love them, I cannot trust you with their lives."

Right there, on a sidewalk in my own neighborhood, under tremendous conviction of the Holy Spirit, I cried out to Him to make my heart more like His.

Preaching the truth without love is like giving someone a good kiss when you have bad breath. No matter how good your kiss is, all the recipient will remember is your bad breath! This is what happens when, in anger or disgust, we tell the lost how terrible and depraved their lives are and how they are surely going to hell. Even though this may be true, our negative approach blocks and distorts the central message of the Bible: that God sent His Son, not to condemn the world, but to save it (see John 3:17).

Reason #2: If we bless the lost, we will stop cursing them. We do not realize how often we curse others, or else we would not do it. When we say, "The lady across the street is a drunkard; she is going to die of cirrhosis of the liver," we are cursing her. When we point to rowdy teenagers and complain, "They are nuisances and morons who drink and drive and experiment with drugs, and soon they are going to kill themselves," we are cursing them. When we pronounce blessings on our neighbors, our city is edified (see Prov. 11:11). But when we curse our neighbors, we tear down the city, beginning with the block we live on.

Reason #3: We speak peace in order to neutralize the demons that have been assigned to blind our neighbors to the light of the gospel. The Bible explains clearly why all the people in our circle of influence have not yet come to the Lord: "The god of this world [the devil] has blinded the minds of the unbelieving, that they might not see the light of the gospel" (2 Cor. 4:4). This means that the devil is *actively* blinding them, because light cannot be blocked passively. Given the fact that Satan is not omnipresent—he cannot be in more than one place at a time—how then can he blind the minds of billions of people simultaneously? He uses demons as implied in the parable of the sower, where we are told that after the seed is planted, the birds of the sky (representing the devil and his forces) come and steal it (see Luke 8:5,12).

The apostle Paul places the task of opening the eyes of the lost squarely on our shoulders and within a context of evangelism and spiritual warfare:

> I am sending you to them to open their eyes and turn them from darkness to light, and from the power of Satan to God (Acts 26:17,18, *NIV*).

Paul leaves no doubt as to the active role Satan and his demons play in blinding the lost to the gospel. Hence, we need to factor in how to disable the demonic grip on those we are trying to reach.

To deal effectively with our spiritual foes, we cannot empower them by approaching the lost in anger. The Bible clearly teaches that our unresolved anger gives room to the devil inside our circle of influence (see Eph. 4:26,27). Our curses will only strengthen the demonic grip on the ones we are trying to save. To reverse this situation, we must renounce our anger and begin to speak peace to the lost.

Blessings are more powerful than curses because curses can be broken. In the celestial poker game, a hand of bless-

BLESSINGS ARE MORE POWERFUL THAN CURSES BECAUSE CURSES CAN BE BROKEN. IN THE CELESTIAL POKER GAME, A HAND OF BLESSINGS ALWAYS BEATS A HAND OF CURSES.

ings always beats a hand of curses. An atmosphere of blessings weakens the grip of demons, and they soon fold and leave the table.

A Tangible Peace

When we speak blessings over those in our circle of influence, sooner or later people who used to avoid us will begin to seek us out, opening the door to fellowship (step 2 in the process). This is because they can actually feel the blessings we have spoken over them. Jesus described this kind of peace as something almost tangible:

> First say, "Peace be to this house." And if a man of peace
> is there, your peace will rest upon him; but if not, it will
> return to you (Luke 10:5,6).

Your neighbors may come to you and say something like, "When I see you walking by, I get a positive vibration." That's New Age lingo for peace. What they mean is that in your presence they feel something tangible—and they like it!

A Christian lady in England had not been able to meet her neighbor, who was bedridden due to a serious condition. Nevertheless, every Thursday she and other believing women spoke peace to her from across the street. This went on for several months until one day, the unbelieving neighbor and her children showed up at the Christian woman's door unexpectedly. The neighbor said, "I came to thank you for the blessings you sent my way, because thanks to those blessings, I am healed." The surprised Christian asked how she knew about the blessings. "Oh, I felt them coming every week. Please, tell me more about it." It took no effort at all to lead that lady and her children to Christ.

If I accidentally cut somebody off on the freeway, I can often feel the other driver's silent curses, even if he or she does not make any obscene gestures or give me an angry blast from the car horn. I feel it first on the back of my neck and then inside as my "soul climate" takes a turn for the worse. If a child of God can feel a curse that is energized by the powers of darkness, how much more will the lost feel a blessing that is empowered by the blood that Jesus shed at Calvary? This is why when we bless our neighbors, they will begin to come around—because they *feel* blessed. Sinners loved to hang around Jesus, because there was just something about Him that drew others to Him. Our neighbors should feel the same way about us, as we are His representatives on Earth (see Luke 10:16).

Two-Way Fellowship

Once you have broken the ice with your neighbors, do not rush to share the gospel with them. Fellowship is the next step, not proclamation. Proclamation is the last step. If you've invited these formerly neglected sinners over for dinner, do not ambush them with the Four Spiritual Laws between the hamburgers and the apple pie. Be patient. You may wonder, *What value is there in fellowship with the lost unless I share the gospel with them?* Fellowship provides an opportunity to show unconditional acceptance by welcoming our neighbors just the way they are instead of the way we want them to be.

So often, we come off decidedly un-Christlike in our interaction with the lost, especially with those who are certified, industrial-strength sinners. We barely put up with them, and we make it painfully clear that we can't wait for them to change and become more like us. This is a destructive attitude unworthy of Christ and His kingdom. To change this, we must spend time with our neighbors, not to patronize or proselytize them but to *receive* from them: "Stay in that house, eating and drinking what they give you" (Luke 10:7). Jesus instructs us to eat and drink everything our neighbors set before us. His evangelism model calls for two-way fellowship, with an emphasis on receiving rather than unilaterally giving.

One of the worst mistakes we make when evangelizing is to treat the unsaved like dirt, as if they have no value whatsoever unless they become Christians. Besides being wrong, this attitude is also very demeaning and only widens the gap between them and us. Worse yet, it widens the chasm between them and Jesus, whom we represent.

Jesus always treated sinners with respect. The worse the sinners—e.g., Zaccheus or the adulterous woman—often the greater the respect with which He treated them. Therefore, we should never treat the lost as people without value. Regardless of how they rate as sinners, the lost always have value as human beings because *they too were made in the image of God.*

Two-way fellowship points us in the right direction. When we allow unbelievers to do something for us, we affirm their value and dignity as God's design and creation. In Jesus' day, the custom was to offer food and lodging to visitors, even to strangers. Today playing football, sharing a meal, working in the yard together or organizing a multifamily garage sale together allows us to speak blessings upon our neighbors at close range.

Fishing Requires Patience

Blessing sinners opens the door to fellowship, and fellowship eventually leads to the third step: an opportunity to meet their felt needs. This will only happen after they trust us enough to disclose those needs. Once such trust exists, they may share that their marriage looks good on the surface but is rotting inside. They may tell us about their fear of losing their job, or they may seek our help with an addiction they cannot overcome. The once-distant neighbors will begin to share heart-to-heart with us because they sense that we have an answer. And they will ask for our help because they now have tangible proof that we truly care for them.

It is at that precise moment when we can say to them, "I have been praying for you, and I would be delighted to pray about this, too." Now you may be thinking, *Shouldn't we lead them to the Lord first?* Understand, what our neighbors are sharing at this point in time is the need they feel is most important—in other words, their felt needs. Obviously, the most important need they have is salvation, but they don't know that yet. Nevertheless, through their felt needs, God creates an avenue to show them that Jesus is indeed a friend of sinners and He came to save them and not to condemn them.

What if I pray and nothing happens? you may wonder. *I don't want God's reputation to be damaged.* If you insist on knowing for sure that God will answer before you decide to pray, you are missing the point. You are only promising prayer, not an answer to prayer. Prayer is the most tangible trace of eternity in the human heart. When you pray for their felt needs, you touch your neighbors at the deepest level, the heart level. This is the closest you can get to them. Sooner or later that touch will register with them. Be patient. Even a master fisherman cannot force the fish to bite. Fishing requires patience.

Our fear that God will get a bad name because of unanswered prayers is unwarranted since unbelievers, at the most rudimentary level, understand prayer better than we do! They know they have a problem for which they have no solution. They suspect that someone greater and more powerful has the answer, but they do not know how to reach such a person. That is why an offer of prayer in a moment of crisis is *always* welcome, because it makes the connection between those two points in their thinking.

Suppose you have a problem that only the president of the United States can fix. He is the person with the power and the resources to solve your dilemma, but you do not know the man, and he does not know you. You can think of no way to make your need known to him. Then, in your most desperate hour, I tell you I have a very good friend who happens to be the head janitor at the White House and he cleans the Oval Office every day. I then propose that if you write a letter to the president about your need, I will give it to my friend to put on the president's desk. If I were to do that, would you say, "Well, Ed, before I sit down to write that letter, you must assure me that the president will read the letter and grant my request. Unless you promise me that he will, I will not write it"? You would never respond this way simply because you would be appreciative that I had reached out to you with a potential solution when you had none.

Unbelievers have the same attitude about prayer. They know that God has a solution, but they do not have His phone number. If you are willing to make the phone call on their behalf, they will be most grateful for it, regardless of the outcome—especially if it is on your dime.

God's Priorities

Furthermore, God seems to be partial to the needs of unbelievers. As I shared in my previous book, our greatest surprise in Resistencia, Argentina, was how quickly and often unexpectedly God answered prayers on behalf of the lost. Sometimes His responses baffled us. A local congregation was praying for one of its members who had terminal cancer. At the same time, the church was praying for an unbeliever who was also dying of cancer. The Christian died and the unbeliever was healed. Someone in the congregation became very upset, claiming it was not fair and asking God for an explanation. The Lord responded, "Let me explain it to you. The believer who died is here with Me in heaven; but if the unbeliever had died, he would be in hell now." Obviously, God has his priorities straight. Let us emulate Him!

Safe to Approach

Once we have completed the first three steps—blessing, fellowship and taking care of their needs—leading our neighbors to the Lord becomes as easy as angling a whale in a swimming pool. You cannot miss because you have given them peace, which is what unbelievers lack the most; you have provided them with the most protective, healing fellowship they have ever enjoyed; and you have offered prayers for needs they feel very deeply and have not been able to meet on their own. Now it is very natural for them to ask, "Tell me, who is this God who loves me?" They feel safe in approaching you because there has been a gradual improvement in the spiritual climate of your relationship as it moved from step one to step four.

We will learn more about changing a spiritual climate in the next chapter. In the meantime, let us review the four steps Jesus laid out for us in Luke 10 and how these steps lead from one to the next:

1. *Blessing* opens the door to unbiased fellowship.
2. *Fellowship* establishes a level of trust, allowing our neighbors to share with us their felt needs.
3. *Prayer* addresses their felt needs.

4. When we intercede for our neighbors, *the kingdom of God comes near them* in a tangible way: "Say to them, 'The kingdom of God has come near to you'" (Luke 10:9).

Please notice that we are not to bring them into the Kingdom; we are to take the Kingdom to them.

Taking the Kingdom to the lost is like driving through the desert in an air-conditioned truck stocked with cold drinks. When you spot a weary pedestrian lost on a lonely road on a hot summer day, if you pull up next to him, you don't need to beg him to come on board. All you need to do is pull over near to him and open the door!

Why Are We Doing Such a Poor Job of Reaching the Lost?

In John 14:12, Jesus tells us that if we believe in Him, we will do greater works than He did while on the earth. This is a key passage, since it provides the answer to a most difficult question: Why is the Church today doing such a poor job of fulfilling the Great Commission compared to the Early Church?

The Early Church was able to fill the entire city of Jerusalem with the teachings of Jesus in just a few weeks (see Acts 5:28). This could not have been an easy task in the city where Jesus was publicly hung as a criminal and His resurrection discredited by rumors cleverly orchestrated and sustained by the religious power brokers. Nevertheless, Jerusalem was reached, and soon the gospel spread to all Judea and Samaria and beyond until "all who lived in Asia heard the word of the Lord" (Acts 19:10).

Furthermore, Paul saturated with the gospel an even greater area—from Jerusalem to Illyricum, across the Adriatic Sea from modern-day Italy—so much so that he had to move on to newer and distant regions, such as Spain, because he was determined not to evangelize where Christ had already been proclaimed (see Rom. 15:19-23). Just consider for a moment the implication of this statement. This means that from Jerusalem in the Middle East all the way to Southern Europe, *there was not a single place where Christ had not been proclaimed.*

THE EARLY CHURCH KNEW SOMETHING THAT WE HAVE NOT YET LEARNED: THEY COULD DO GREATER WORKS THAN JESUS DID.

Moreover, this extraordinary expansion of the faith happened in a relatively short time in the face of fierce and brutal persecution and without the abundance of resources available to us today. What's more, history tells us that by the beginning of the fourth century, Christians had "conquered" the mighty empire that had taken pleasure in persecuting them. How did this come about? The Early Church knew something that we have not yet learned: *They could do greater works than Jesus did.*

The Command to Do Greater Things

How can we possibly do something greater than the Son of God has done? Many Bible commentaries are silent or evasive on this topic. Others attempt to sidestep the issue by saying that although we can never surpass the *quality* of Jesus' works, we can certainly exceed them in *quantity*. After all, Jesus preached publicly for only three years, and He never preached to more than a few thousand people at a time. Billy Graham and others have led international ministries that spanned decades, sometimes preaching to hundreds of thousands in a single gathering. Jesus never traveled far from Galilee during His ministry, whereas many believers have since carried the gospel to the nations of the world, thus having done something greater than Jesus. These are nice suggestions, but they represent awful hermeneutics because they have nothing to do with what the text actually says:

> Truly, truly, I say to you, he who believes in Me, the works that I do shall he do also; and greater works than these shall he do; because I go to the Father. And whatever you ask in My name, that I will do, that the Father may be glorified in the Son. If you ask Me anything in My name, I will do it. *If you love Me, you will keep My commandments* (John 14:12-15, emphasis added).

Jesus states that everyone who believes in Him should do the same works that He did. And now that He has been glorified, these works have been upgraded to *greater* works. This point cannot be argued at all. It is a promise dependent on one condition: belief in Jesus. If we believe in Jesus, we are not only entitled to do greater works than He did; we are *commanded* to do so.

What are the greater works Jesus commands us to do? His own words suggest that they have to do with prayer: "And whatever you ask in My name, that I will do, that the Father may be glorified in the Son" (v. 13). He is not speaking about prayer in general, however, but rather about a specific kind of prayer: prayer that addresses the felt needs of the lost. How do I arrive at this conclusion? The key is the word "glorified." Jesus says that He will do anything we ask in His name, so that the Father will be glorified in the Son. That is, unbelievers will come to the

Father through Jesus when they have been convinced of His divinity by a miracle.

Philip: A Prototype of Modern Man

To see this more clearly, we need to go back to a few moments earlier in this same conversation, when Jesus says to His disciples, "Believe in God, believe also in Me" (John 14:1). In other words, "Believe also that I am God." The disciples are probably stunned at this point, but Jesus goes on, making yet another amazing, absolutely unprecedented statement: "In My Father's house are many dwelling places. I am going ahead to prepare a place for you. When those dwellings are ready, I will come and take you there myself" (see vv. 2,3). This is an extraordinary promise because up to this moment (as recorded in the Bible), never have mortal, sinful men been so openly and clearly assured of going to heaven. When Thomas asks how to get to this wonderful place, Jesus declares, "I am the way, and the truth, and the life; no one comes to the Father, but through Me" (v. 6).

Jesus then comforts His disciples, assuring them that because they have known Him, they have known God and have seen Him. Philip now chimes in, saying, "Lord, show us the Father, and it is enough for us" (v. 8).

Philip was probably a shy person. I say this because shy people make good diplomats; they are able to say something negative in such a way that it sounds positive. Philip says something here that on the surface sounds polite and humble but in reality is rude and negative: "Lord, if you show me the Father, that is enough for me." But Jesus is able to see through his veneer to the core of unbelief behind Philip's comment. This is why He confronts Philip, demanding, "Why don't you believe Me when I say that he who has seen Me has seen the Father?" (see vv. 9,10). Knowing that

Philip does not believe in His divinity, Jesus says, "Philip, if you do not believe in Me by My words, believe in Me by My works. Let My miracles prove to you that I am who I say" (see v. 11).

Philip believed in God, and he wanted to go to a better place—the Father's house—when he died. Today, the vast majority of the population claims to believe in God, and they would love to go to a better place when they die; but like Philip, most of them do not believe that Jesus is the only way to the Father. That is why this passage merits attention and serious study. If we understand how Jesus dealt with this issue that affects so many people in this day and age, we will have the key to reaching our cities for Christ.

What Jesus is teaching Philip is that it is all right to see in order to believe. Jesus knows that Philip, once convinced, will do "the works that I do" and "greater works than these"—miracles worked through prayer—to convince others who likewise do not believe that Jesus is God or the way to God (v. 12).

This passage is extraordinary in that it presents prayer and evangelism as fully integrated components of the same equation. Traditionally, the Church has used prayer as a primer for evangelism. We have prayed for the lost so that, when evangelized, they will listen and hopefully receive Jesus. In this passage, however, Jesus presents prayer *as* evangelism. Prayer becomes evangelism when used to open the eyes of unbelievers to the divinity of Jesus. To that effect, He used someone like Philip, who did not believe that Jesus is God, to show us how to break through this widespread barrier of unbelief. The key is *prayer for miracles that meet the felt needs of unbelieving people.*

A Practical Exercise

Let's test this principle of prayer evangelism in a hypothetical setting.

Imagine yourself standing at the front door of your house. Now, count five neighboring houses to the right, five to the left and another five across from or behind your house. If you live in an apartment building, identify five families to your right and five to your left and another five on the floors above you or below you. Essentially, you have identified a cluster of families comprising roughly a hundred people. Now focus on the most needy of these households and identify its most vulnerable member. Most likely you are going to come up with somebody who is depressed, terminally ill, perennially bankrupt or controlled and being destroyed by vices. Now picture that person in the midst of a major crisis, when everything is caving in and causing him or her to become desperate. Now imagine yourself going up to that person and saying, "Please, do not worry. I am praying for you in the name of Jesus for God to intervene on your behalf." Startled, that person may say to you, "Oh, don't waste your time because I don't believe in prayer," to which you would reply, "Oh, don't worry. It doesn't make any difference whether you believe in prayer or not since you are not praying. I am the one praying, and I believe in prayer." This person may retort, "I do not believe in Jesus either." You then say, "Don't worry. Once I am done, you will."

At this point, it is fair to say that you are making that neighbor an offer that he or she cannot refuse—an offer very similar to the one Jesus made to Philip: "If you do not believe in Me by My words, believe in Me by My works." Now imagine that after you have prayed for a miracle, a miracle does happen! The house that was in foreclosure is miraculously saved through an extraordinary series of events, or a better job replaces the one that was lost, or a sick person is healed. Would that person suddenly be interested in knowing who Jesus is? Absolutely!

Stick with a Winning Strategy

Most of us, if not all of us, came to the Lord as a result of someone's prayers. Why then do we discard this winning strategy once we have become doctrinally and theologically educated? If we are going to fulfill the Great Commission in our generation, we need to find a better way to reach the lost. Prayer evangelism means doing greater works than Jesus did. It's exhilarating, edifying and exciting, and this method accomplishes much more than any other, as we will soon see.

MOST OF US CAME TO THE LORD AS A RESULT OF SOMEONE'S PRAYERS. WHY DISCARD A WINNING STRATEGY?

Never before has the Church had more money, training and members than it has today; yet never has the Church done a poorer job in reaching the lost, proportionate to those resources. Why? Because we have been busy doing *lesser* works instead of *greater* works than Jesus did.

Imagine two airplanes circling over your city, each one carrying a large sum of money in its cargo bay. One of the planes is carrying $1 million in American pennies, or one-cent coins. The other plane carries the same amount in $1,000 bills. Both planes dump their cargo over the city, leaving $2 million scattered on the ground. You immediately organize two teams to see which one will collect a million dollars first. However, Team A confines their efforts to collecting only pennies, whereas Team B sets out to collect $1,000 bills.

Which team will be noisier, take up more space, become more frustrated and end up writing books to explain why it can't be done? Team A, right? Yes, because they must find 100 million pennies to reach the goal. Team B, on the other hand, needs to find only a thousand $1,000 bills to complete its task.

The Church needs to switch strategies. We must learn how to do greater works than Jesus did. And doing those works means praying for the felt needs of unbelievers and expecting miracles that will prove to them Jesus is the Son of God.

A Method for Reaching Cities

The apostle Paul also teaches about prayer evangelism in 1 Timothy 2:1-8, where he admonishes us to pray for everyone everywhere. However, to fully comprehend what Paul is talking about, we need to look at the context established in verse 15 of the previous chapter.

As you and I read our Bibles, it is easy to assume that the chapter divisions are divinely inspired. This is not so. Except for the collected Psalms, the Holy Spirit did not divide any of the books into chapters. The insertion of chapter breaks was done by man and, sadly, these are often misleading. This is why 1 Timothy 2:1-8 is often thought to contain instructions on how to conduct prayer meetings in private. However, if we ignore the chapter division and begin to read in chapter 1, verse 15, we will see this passage in a different and far more exciting light.

Paul writes, "It is a trustworthy statement, deserving full acceptance, that Christ Jesus came into the world to save sinners" (v. 15). Paul is saying: "Timothy, this statement is so reliable that you can bank on it—that once exposed to it, everybody in your city is going to accept it." He is not saying that everybody will accept Jesus but, rather, that everybody will accept the truth that He came to save sinners. Paul is talking about the lost in

Timothy's city, and he uses this statement as a preface to introduce a method for reaching all of them.

We often miss the evangelistic nature and focus of Paul's teaching because, moved by the realization that he is the greatest of sinners (see v. 16), Paul takes a praise detour: "Now to the King eternal, immortal, invisible, the only God, be honor and glory for ever and ever. Amen" (1 Tim. 1:17). Unfortunately, some Bible editors see the word "amen" and wrongly assume that it provides a natural break in the text. As a result, many Bibles include a subtitle before the next verse, leaving us with the impression that Paul changes subjects. This is not the case.

In verse 18, Paul directs Timothy to keep a certain commandment that he may fight the good fight. What is the good fight? The good fight, in this context, is not so much a matter of personal growth but, rather, the struggle to open the eyes of the lost to the fact that Jesus came into the world to save them. Paul is talking here about a strategy for reaching the lost; he is explain-ing to Timothy how to reach a city or a region for Christ.

Which One Is the Command?

To equip Timothy to do this Paul gives him a command: "This command I entrust to you, Timothy, my son . . . [so that] you may fight the good fight" (v. 18). Upon reading this we immediately begin to look for the command. Unfortunately, we wrongly conclude that the command can be found in one of only two verses, since chapter 1 is fast coming to an end. We discard verse 20, as it refers to Hymeneus and Alexander, who obviously had disobeyed the command. So we look to verse 19: "Keeping faith and a good conscience." This is the command, right? To have a clean conscience in which to store up faith, because if we have faith nothing will be impossible for us?

No, Paul does not say, "*Keep* the faith and *keep* a good con-science," which is how one gives a command. Instead, Paul uses the verb form "keeping." We never tell our children, "*Going* to bed, *doing* your homework, and *being* nice to your brother." No! We tell them, "*Go* to bed now, *do* your homework promptly, and *be* nice to your brother or else." Paul is not giving a com-mand in verse 19 but is describing the context in which the command is to be obeyed. He is saying to carry out the com-mand from a position of holiness—thus the need for a clean conscience.

To find out what Paul's command is, we need to look to the next chapter:

> First of all, then, I urge that entreaties and prayers, peti-tions and thanksgivings, be made on behalf of all men (1 Tim. 2:1).

The expressions "first of all" and "I urge" are intended to set the stage for the enunciation of something that should not be over-looked—obviously a command. What Paul is commanding is that the Church pray for everybody, everywhere. Why? Because God wants everybody to be saved:

> This is good and acceptable in the sight of God our Savior, who desires all men to be saved and to come to the knowledge of the truth (vv. 3,4).

The compelling evidence for the evangelistic nature of the pas-sage that begins in 1 Timothy 1:15 is undeniable.

Paul tells Timothy that by mobilizing the Church to pray for everybody in the city, they will ensure that all sinners will have an opportunity to know that Jesus came to save them. Paul is talking about organizing systematic prayer for the lost—what we now call prayer evangelism.

Change in the Spiritual Climate

Paul's command also contains a promise:

> I urge that entreaties and prayers, petitions and thanks-givings, be made on behalf of all men, for kings and all who are in authority, in order that we may lead a tranquil and quiet life in all godliness and dignity (1 Tim. 2:1,2).

The apostle indicates that if we pray for everybody, including those who are in authority, we will see a dramatic improvement in the spiritual climate around us; we will be able to live tranquil lives in all godliness. Now, there is no way godliness can increase in our cities unless ungodliness decreases. There is no way we can live in quiet dignity unless our job is done and the good fight is won.

Paul confirms that the key to reaching the lost is to provide them with tangible proof that Jesus came to save them by meeting their felt needs through prayer—prayer as evangelism. This is how to reach cities the way the Early Church did it: not by relying on the skills of a few but by the whole Church's modeling the whole gospel to the whole city through prayerful evangelism.

Text Without Its Context Is Only a Pretext

Go therefore and make disciples of all the nations, baptizing them in the name of the Father and the Son and the Holy Spirit (Matt. 28:19).

Reaching entire regions becomes feasible when we reexamine the Great Commission through the lens of prayer evangelism.

Let us take a closer look at Matthew 28:19. Here we see a command to go to all the nations to preach the gospel to everybody, to baptize them and to teach them everything Jesus taught us. This is a very tall order, to say the least. Who can do this and still hold a demanding secular job? Or be a good father or mother or even a pastor, with the time demands each of these roles entails? Time and again, we find ourselves torn between the need to be a witness in the place where we are planted and the command to go someplace else to reach the lost. The hard reality is that after nearly 2,000 years of trying, we have not gotten the job done, since perhaps half of the world's population has yet to hear that Jesus came to save all men.

Worse, a great number of those yet to be reached live in our cities—quite a few live in our own neighborhoods—and they show no signs of being reached anytime soon. What a tragedy! Why have we failed so miserably? The reason is that we have taken Matthew 28:19, the verse we consider to be at the heart of the Great Commission, out of context and, in so doing, we have developed a faulty methodology.

A text without its context becomes a pretext. When we look at this verse isolated from its context, the weight of fulfilling the Great Commission comes to rest exclusively on our shoulders. Our traditional understanding of this text is that it is *we* who must go and do the evangelizing, the teaching and the baptizing of so many. This is a crushing weight.

Now let us view this passage in its context by adding the two verses that precede and follow it:

And Jesus came up and spoke to them, saying, "*All authority has been given to Me in heaven and on earth.* Go therefore and make disciples of all the nations, baptizing them in the name of the Father and the Son and the Holy Spirit, teaching them to observe all that I commanded you; and lo, *I am with you always*, even to the end of the age" (Matt. 28:18-20, emphasis added).

Now, two powerful new components have come into the picture: First, Jesus has authority *everywhere*, in heaven and on Earth. This means there is not a single problem He cannot take care of or a single need He cannot meet. Second, He is with us all the time. If we replace "go" with "going," as it appears in the original Greek, we see a dramatic shift in responsibility. Now the weight is no longer on our shoulders but is placed on the broad, matchless shoulders of Jesus. Jesus is saying, "As you go about your daily life, you will come across people who have needs. Just remember two things: I can take care of them, and I am right there next to you." How are we supposed to engage Him to meet their needs? "Ask Me anything in My name, [and] I will do it" (John 14:14). He is saying, "Don't just talk about Me. Introduce Me to the lost by showing them my wonders."

Jesus is not merely a message to be preached; He is a proactive Savior. He is ready to prove to the lost that He came into the world to save sinners by performing miracles when they need them the most. This is the heart of prayer evangelism and, when properly implemented, it is capable of doing much more than leading a few neighbors to the Lord. Prayer evangelism can change the spiritual climate over entire cities and regions.

Note
1. Beverly Jaime and her husband, David, are associate pastors at Cathedral of Faith in San Jose, California.

How to Change the Spiritual Climate

Changing the climate is not unknown to us.
Our problem is that we do not believe that the same climate we
have in church can and should be all over the city.

Climate determines much about how people live each day. If the temperature goes down 20 degrees on an autumn afternoon, many people reach for sweaters. If it begins to rain, people grab their raincoats and umbrellas. Weather affects a lot of what goes on around us.

Central heating is not necessary in the Caribbean, but it is a definite must in Alaskan homes and offices. On the other hand, sunscreen is in not heavy demand in Greenland, but most of us would not dare venture into the Sahara Desert without it. You will not find many citrus farmers in Boston, whereas one would soon go broke trying to make his living as a fisherman in Albuquerque.

Climate indeed plays a large part in where we choose to live, how we dress, what we eat and which recreational activities we participate in. But consider the profound effect that a *spiritual* climate has on our cities. A godly climate allows people to lead "a tranquil and quiet life in all godliness and dignity" (1 Tim. 2:2). The *King James Version* promises a "quiet and peaceable life in all godliness and honesty." Lack of godliness in a city produces quite the opposite.

What Can We Do About It?

We have no problem believing that it is possible to change the spiritual climate inside a home, in a church building or even at a stadium during a crusade. Every Sunday in church we see the climate change gradually as the service proceeds. The concept of changing a spiritual climate is not foreign to us.

However, we do have a problem believing that the same climate we enjoy in church can and should be enjoyed all over the city. Yet this is promised in 1 Timothy 2:1-9, where Paul tells us that if we pray for everybody, everywhere, we will be able to live quiet and tranquil lives in all godliness and honesty. For godliness to increase in a city, ungodliness must decrease, and none of this can happen without radical improvement in the spiritual climate of the city.

For far too long, we have left control of the spiritual climate in our cities in the hands of the devil. This is evident when we look around at the mire of sin, the hostility and anger, the criminal activity and the crushing weight of hopelessness on our fellow citizens. Every week thousands in our cities get married, hoping for a bright future; and every week a similar number watch their marriages disintegrate. Satan is keeping a subzero climate in place, while the Church is rubbing sticks together, trying to spark a few fires to keep its own people from freezing.

But what if the Church in the city was able to take control of the spiritual thermostat away from the devil and set it to a comfortable 70°F? Suddenly, Satan would be on the defensive, assigning demons to frantically distribute melting ice cubes around the city in a futile attempt to bring the temperature down a few degrees.

When the pastors repented at the gates of the city in San Nicolas, Argentina (see chapter 1), I expected good things to come out of it; but I was not prepared for how *much* good came of it or for how quickly it happened. The unprecedented media acceptance, the warm welcome by secular authorities, the support from the Catholic church for our city-reaching efforts, the friendly reception during the door-to-door visitation and especially the miracles at the prayer fair were all extraordinary in the extreme. All of this took place because the spiritual climate over the city had been changed.

The Witch That Switched

The change in climate became dramatically evident when a witch's coven became a lighthouse of prayer in *less than 60 minutes*. This is how it happened. During the radio broadcast designed to launch lighthouses of prayer in San Nicolas, members of the international prayer delegation went to several different homes to listen to and participate in the radio broadcast. The visitors and their hosts had a great time as everyone was guided through a bilingual radio prayer exercise.

However, two of the international delegates, totally unaware, went to the wrong house! They knocked on the door and a very strange looking lady opened it. When they asked, in broken Spanish, if hers was a house of prayer, the woman replied affirmatively in a very spooky voice. Unsure of themselves, they went in, turned on their radios and became connected to the Church that was praying all over the city. They soon found out that they were indeed in a house of prayer—*a house of prayer to Satan*. Their hostess was a witch and her house home to a witch's coven.

Demons manifested in their presence but were quickly cast out. Within the hour, the witch received the Lord and was filled with the Holy Spirit. Her two daughters also received the Lord and, for the balance of the broadcast, the host and her unexpected visitors rid the house of all satanic paraphernalia. What used to be a satanic stronghold became God's outpost. Under ordinary circumstances, Satan would have had the upper hand, home field advantage, if you will—but not this time, because the spiritual climate had changed. That night the Church was in control of the city.

Can I Be Your Son Again?

This is not an isolated case. Let me share two stories of what happened when a similar three-day launch of prayer lighthouses was held in Modesto, California. On Monday night, the night of the first radio broadcast, a couple invited their backslidden son to join them to dedicate their home as a lighthouse of prayer. The son refused, slammed the door and left, visibly upset. He spent the night someplace else, while the parents went ahead with the dedication. The next day they sanctified their home. As part of this process they were led to forgive those who had offended them. In the closing minutes of the broadcast, they were directed to lift up holy hands, without anger or dissension, and to pray for someone who needed a touch from God. They prayed for God to touch their son, wherever he was.

Where was he? He was in bed with a woman who was not his wife, committing adultery—not the most spiritually conducive environment, I should say. Nevertheless, he felt God's touch in that place. He apologized to the lady for his sudden loss of focus, got dressed in a hurry and called home, begging permission to go back. He rededicated his life to the Lord, and the next day he joined his parents in prayer walking their neighborhood!

The following is another extraordinary testimony from that week. On Tuesday evening, Doug was in his apartment waiting for the radio broadcast to begin. The topic of the broadcast was sanctification of the home, and he was looking forward to it. Several years earlier Doug had married a woman who had a child, a boy, from a previous marriage. Doug adopted the boy as his son and, later, God blessed the married couple with a boy and two daughters of their own. Unfortunately, the marriage ended in divorce, and when it did, Doug renounced the adoption, which devastated the young man. They had not seen each other in the 11 years since.

Five minutes into the broadcast, Doug's ex-son knocked on the door, burst into the apartment and poured out a litany of pain caused by failure after failure. Doug easily led him to the Lord but then realized that the young man would not have been in such a condition had he not rejected him. Immediately, Doug begged his forgiveness. The ex-son forgave him and then, in a trembling voice, he asked, "Could you ever forgive me for what I did to your daughters?" This was a most difficult issue because when Doug rejected him, the young man had abused them out of spite. Moved, Doug told him that he did forgive him, and both

WHEN THE SPIRITUAL
CLIMATE CHANGES
FOR THE BETTER, SO
DOES EVERYBODY AND
EVERYTHING IN
THE CITY.

fell into a warm embrace, tears running down their cheeks. In this tender setting the young man asked, "Doug, can I become your son again?" Doug assented and right there, in prayer, he readopted the young man. Afterwards, they prayed together for Doug's natural son to receive the Lord. The following Monday, Doug's natural son asked to go with him to an evangelistic meeting, where he publicly received the Lord!

Each of these cases represents an extraordinary outpouring of the power of God, something we seldom see in our neopagan, postmodern world. The reason for these breakthroughs is that the spiritual climate over the city had changed. When the spiritual climate changes for the better, so does *everybody* and *everything* in the city.

At what point in time did the climate radically change? It happened on Wednesday evening, right after the city had been prayer walked.

I'll Meet You at the Prayer Fair

In San Nicolas, where this weeklong process was pioneered, we met Wednesday morning with the pastors to strategize, and the Lord specifically instructed us *not* to engage any demons that evening but to concentrate exclusively on speaking peace to every home we walked by. By the end of the evening the entire city had been *silently* prayer walked, every home *quietly* blessed and an invitation *surreptitiously* placed under every door, inviting people to a prayer fair the following Saturday. On Thursday and Friday, pastors and intercessors spent the days in prayer and fasting. On Saturday morning, every home in town was visited with tremendous results.

We knocked on doors and asked, "Do you know that today is the favorable year of the Lord?" Most people pleaded ignorance. When asked if they knew what this meant, none of them had the slightest idea. We told them that "favorable" meant that God wanted to do them a favor. When asked if they needed a favor, most of them said yes. They were then shown a half-page ad in the local newspaper featuring an invitation to the prayer fair. The ad included a coupon good for free admission and unlimited prayers! Everybody received this with pleasure.

At 3 P.M. people began to converge on the prayer fair. Quite a few carried our coupons, and when they stopped at the information counter for directions, the dialogue went something like this:

Inquirer: (showing the coupon) "Where do I go first?"

Believer: "It depends on your problem. What is it?"

Inquirer: "My wife left me."

Believer: (turning toward a billboard) "Let's see. Here it is! Family problems is aisle 5. The ushers (undercover intercessors) will lead you there."

Once they got to aisle 5 or 2 or 3, depending on their need, intercessors and pastors prayed for them. God touched inquirers all over the park, and as soon as they felt His power, they wanted to know more about Jesus. Many received the Lord right then and there.

In retrospect, this kind of looks like a sure thing; but when we were preparing for it, lacking prior experience and the solid biblical foundation we have now, we were not so certain. I remember wondering on Thursday and Friday if *anyone* would come to the prayer fair. My worry was in vain. On Saturday crowds eagerly came to the park and miracles took place. The spiritual climate was so good that everyone, it seemed, was able to lead someone to the Lord.

When that historic week was over, I asked the Lord to show me the biblical basis for the dramatic change in spiritual climate we had experienced. He led me to the Gospel of Luke, which I read several times in one sitting. I noticed that Luke documents *two different kinds of climate during the time of Jesus' ministry.* The first 9 chapters of Luke portray a hostile climate in the land; the last 15 show a largely favorable spiritual climate. This change in climate and the reasons behind it are very important for the subject at hand.

Hostile Climate

Early in Jesus' ministry the climate in Galilee and Judea was so unfavorable that in Luke 9:41 Jesus sounded markedly like someone who felt like quitting. He said to His disciples, "O unbelieving and perverted generation, how long shall I be with you, and put up with you?" Obviously, Jesus was quite frustrated and unhappy with them.

By the next chapter, however, He felt entirely different: "He rejoiced greatly in the Holy Spirit" (Luke 10:21), and He began to praise God for what His disciples had done.

If we examine carefully these two phases in Jesus' earthly ministry, we will find the key to changing the spiritual climate over our cities. First we will see how the spiritual climate became progressively worse to the point of being almost unbearable for our Lord.

A Challenge Issued by God

When Jesus emerged from the baptismal waters, the Father declared, "You are My beloved Son; in You I am well pleased"

(Luke 3:22, *NKJV*). This statement was obviously not intended for the benefit of Jesus, since He knew very well who He was and what His Father thought of Him. Nor was it meant for John the Baptist who, a moment earlier, had made a declaration to that effect. Since there is no evidence that the crowd heard the voice from heaven, it is possible that this declaration was intended for the devil himself. By saying, "In You I am well pleased," God was making known to the devil that a *sinless human being* had invaded his kingdom of sin.

This posed a serious threat to Satan, whose rulership was empowered by sin. God reminded the devil that he had no leverage against Jesus because of His holy nature. Satan's kingdom had been invaded, and God's statement—the equivalent of "Go ahead, Satan, make My day"—was the opening bell for the match of the ages.

In response to God's challenge, the devil came to the fore and for 40 days tried to draw Jesus into his control through temptations to sin. Once defeated, the devil "departed from Him until an opportune time" (Luke 4:13). Traditionally, we have identified the next opportune time to be when Jesus was in brutal anguish at the Garden of Gethsemane or on the following day when He was hanging on the cross. However, I believe that the devil did not wait that long to come back at his foe; in fact, he was waiting in ambush right around the corner.

Friends and Neighbors Are Turned Against Him

Jesus returned in the power of the Holy Spirit to His home region of Galilee, and His fame began to spread. While in the town of Nazareth, He taught an audience of friends and neighbors in the synagogue; "and all were speaking well of Him, and wondering at the gracious words which were falling from His lips" (Luke 4:22). In human terms, nothing could have been more positive and affirming.

Suddenly, "all in the synagogue were filled with rage . . . and they rose up and cast Him out of the city, and led Him to the brow of the hill on which their city had been built, in order to throw Him down the cliff" (vv. 28,29). For a hometown crowd to take such a sudden turn from adulation and praise to unrestrained violence against one of their own is, in the *natural* world, psychologically and sociologically improbable in the extreme. Jesus' teaching that day was hardly incendiary. I can only attribute these happenings to the *supernatural* intervention of evil. In other words, this was Satan's next opportune moment, which he seized and turned Jesus' friends and neighbors against Him. As a result, the most sociable man ever to walk on the earth left town knowing He had been rejected by the people He grew up with.

But Satan was not through. From there, Jesus went down to the city of Capernaum, where He taught on the Sabbath in the local synagogue. It was there that He came up against a very aggressive demon—a very disrespectful, Rambo-class demon who challenged Jesus publicly (see Luke 4:34). Jesus cast him out. That same evening, Satan dropped his pistol and took up a machine gun, unleashing many demons, who also were disrespectfully loud and in Jesus' face (see v. 41).

The Pharisees and Scribes Turn Against Jesus

The religious leaders of the nation came out to hear Him preach and, reasoning in their hearts, began speaking out against Him: "Who is this man who speaks blasphemies?" (v. 21). Soon the scribes and the Pharisees attempted to drive a wedge between Jesus and His disciples with their slanderous grumbling.

After Jesus rebuked them, they began to watch Him closely, not to find the truth but "in order that they might find reason to accuse Him" (Luke 6:7). After they were embarrassed in a Sabbath confrontation, the religious leaders became "filled with rage," and they began plotting against Him (v. 11). Theirs was a murderous rage, similar to that experienced by the rioters in Nazareth and undoubtedly satanic in nature.

On the surface their anger may appear to be simply a negative human reaction. However, its satanic origins were exposed by Jesus when, shortly afterwards, He indicted the Pharisees and scribes as murderous on account of their direct connection to the devil: "You are of your father the devil, and you want to do the desires of your father. He was a murderer from the beginning" (John 8:44). This indictment did not make Him any more popular with the religious authorities.

So it was that in a short time the devil had lined up against Him a multitude of demons, His friends and neighbors and the religious establishment. Things would soon get worse.

John the Baptist Is Neutralized

Jesus described His cousin John the Baptist as the greatest man to be born of a woman (see Matt. 11:11). Their mothers had been friends and faith pals while bringing to term supernatural pregnancies. John grew up to become Jesus' front man, who prepared the people for His coming. In a sea of humanity totally blinded to Jesus' message, John represented the only lighthouse of hope, albeit a very bright one.

However, in Luke 7 the spiritual climate had become increasingly hostile, and John had been imprisoned by Herod for speaking out against the ruler's public sinfulness. Confined and awaiting his inevitable execution, John began to have doubts. So

John sent his disciples to inquire of his cousin, "Are you the Expected One, or do we look for someone else?" (Luke 7:19).

I suspect this must have been a most difficult moment for Jesus, for John had also been affected by the Satan-controlled climate.

Nature Is Manipulated Against Jesus

In Luke 8:22-24, the boat in which Jesus and His disciples were sailing was buffeted and nearly sunk by a sudden severe storm. The disciples, most of whom were experienced sailors and fishermen, literally *cried out* in fear—not a very manly reaction, I grant you. Surely they had seen and experienced their share of fierce storms, but these brave men now found themselves fresh out of courage. I submit to you that the reason for this is that *this was a most unusual storm*—a storm unleashed, or at least manipulated, by the devil himself.

When the disciples woke Jesus, "He rebuked the wind and the surging waves, and they stopped, and it became calm" (v. 24). There is no need for the Creator to have to rebuke His creation; rebuking is what Jesus did when He confronted demons. Under natural circumstances, all the Creator would need to do is to tell the wind to subside and the waves to calm down. The fact that He had to rebuke them gives us ample room to speculate that supernatural evil was behind such a fierce storm.

Foreigners Turn Against Jesus

In the region of the Gerasenes, Jesus confronted not one or a few demons but a legion that had terrorized the area while in possession of a local man. Jesus cast them out, set the man free and delivered the region from a serious public menace (Luke 8:26-33).

What happened next does not make much sense in the natural realm, which is why we need to seek answers in the supernatural.

Logically, we might expect that in view of their deliverance from this terror, the locals should have asked Jesus to stay around, if for no other reason than to keep them safe in case the demons returned. They should have expressed their gratitude to Jesus. Instead, "they were gripped with great fear" and "asked Him to depart" (v. 37). Once again, the natural did not come naturally; most likely this abnormal response was also the result of supernatural evil.

I trust that you now see that Jesus operated in a very hostile climate run by the devil himself. But the worst was yet to come: His disciples joined the opposition, too.

The Disciples Sabotage Jesus' Mission

Finally, Jesus' own disciples turned against Him, though perhaps unwittingly. First, the Twelve expressed mild contempt for the crowds whom Jesus loved so much, saying, "Send the multitude away" (Luke 9:12). Then Jesus forbade the Twelve to preach, apparently because they were not willing to deny themselves and humbly follow Him (see Luke 9:21-26), and Peter was rebuked as a mouthpiece for the devil himself (see Matt. 16:23).

Soon after, at the scene of the Transfiguration, Peter, James and John were rebuked by God the Father because of their self-centeredness (see Luke 9:32-36). Meanwhile, the other nine disciples were being defeated by a single demon in the village below (see v. 40). Amazingly, after this series of discouraging events, the disciples got into an argument as to who among them might be the greatest (see v. 46)!

Finally, after Jesus chastised His disciples for hindering someone who was doing what they seemed to be incapable of doing—that is, casting out demons (see Luke 9:50)—James and John offered to command that fire from heaven be sent to consume a village of Samaritans who had turned them away (see v. 54). So Jesus passed a most severe judgment: "You do not know what kind of spirit you are of" (v. 55). In other words, the disciples were under the control of Satan rather than of God.

The closing verses of this sad chapter show Jesus unable to recruit new, committed disciples (see Luke 9:57-62). There is no question that the spiritual climate was absolutely hostile. Jesus, like the Church today, had won every battle; but He was in danger of losing the war. We will look further at the disciples' inefficiency in chapter 7, but it is no wonder that Jesus voiced his frustration with His disciples, calling them "unbelieving and perverted" (v. 42). Obviously, the climate could not have been worse if this was the best He could say about His closest associates.

Then something happened that radically turned the tide in Jesus' favor.

Favorable Climate

A most dramatic change in the spiritual climate is recorded in Luke 10. However, let us first look at the ensuing events that took place in this improved climate, and we will come back to Luke 10 later.

The Disciples Ask to Learn How to Pray

"Lord, teach us to pray" (Luke 11:1). Jesus had repeatedly exhorted His disciples to listen and to learn. Even the Father had to rebuke Peter, James and John, telling them to stop talking and to listen to Jesus instead. The fact that these same "hearing-impaired" men came asking to be taught is indicative of a definite change for the better.

Demonic Activity Virtually Disappears

In the first nine chapters of Luke, we see very aggressive demons rearing their ugly heads all over and in large numbers. However, for the balance of Luke—the next 14 chapters—*only two demons are mentioned*, and neither of them is the aggressive Rambo type. In fact, both demons are so proper, they seem to have graduated from prep school! One is a dumb demon who went away without a peep (see Luke 11:14). The other is a demon who had tormented a woman for 18 years, but Jesus healed her without even addressing the demon (see Luke 13:12).

The virtual absence of demonic activity in the last 14 chapters of Luke is definite proof that the spiritual winds had shifted and that the new climate was not hospitable for demonic activity.

The Multitudes Begin to Increase
Until Everybody Is on Board

"The multitudes marveled. The crowds were increasing" (Luke 11:14,29). Unlike the time when friends, neighbors and foreigners turned against Him, multitudes were instead flocking to Jesus—so much so that He declared, "Everybody is forcing their way into the kingdom of God" (see Luke 16:16). Now that is 100% responsiveness!

Jesus Takes the Offensive

Rather than waiting for the religious leaders to attempt to trap Him with their devious questions, Jesus took the initiative and exposed the leaders of the establishment as frauds (see Luke 11:35-52).

He publicly called them hypocrites: "Beware of the leaven of the Pharisees, which is hypocrisy" (Luke 12:1).

He humiliated them (see Luke 13:17).

His enemies, once so sure of themselves, suddenly realized they were powerless to harm Him as they had planned to when the climate was in their favor. Now they wished that Herod would do something to take care of their problem. But Jesus challenged them *and* Herod publicly: "Go and tell that fox, 'Behold, I cast out demons and perform cures today and tomorrow, and the third day I reach My goal'" (Luke 13:32). Jesus was telling the Pharisees, "There is nothing that either you or Herod can do to Me. I *will* fulfill My mission."

The Pharisees, always a very outspoken and opinionated bunch, were now silenced: "They were watching Him closely. . . . But they kept silent. . . . They could make no reply" (Luke 14:1, 4,6). They were reduced to grumbling and scoffing (see Luke 15:2; 16:14), very inane and impotent actions for a proud group that had been, until recently, making plans to kill Jesus.

Jesus' Army Is on the March and Adding New Recruits

His disciples came to Him and asked for their faith to be increased, a very healthy request (see Luke 17:5). Whereas in the past they would argue or ignore Jesus, now when confronted with an assignment, they ask for tools (faith) to carry it out.

About this time, Jesus added children to His army, calling them role models for His followers:

And they were bringing even their babies to Him so that He might touch them. . . . Jesus called for them, saying,

"Permit the children to come to Me, and do not hinder them, for the kingdom of God belongs to such as these. Truly I say to you, whoever does not receive the kingdom of God like a child shall not enter it at all" (Luke 18:15-17).

Later at Jericho, a poor blind man was healed, and an entire town was won over:

And Jesus said to him, "Receive your sight; your faith has made you well." And immediately he regained his sight, and began following Him, glorifying God; and when all the people saw it, they gave praise to God (Luke 18:42,43).

A Most Decisive Chapter

In Luke 19, Satan suffered a major setback when Jesus won over one of his best players, Zaccheus, a chief tax collector and a man so despised that he was considered beyond redemption by his fellow citizens (see Luke 19:2-9). With the devil's game plan now in tatters, Jesus began running up the score.

Multitudes flocked to Him from all over and, having become His disciples, they took an active role in His mission:

The whole multitude of the disciples began to praise God joyfully with a loud voice for all the miracles which they had seen, saying, "BLESSED IS THE KING WHO COMES IN THE NAME OF THE LORD; Peace in heaven and glory in the highest!" (vv. 37,38).

When the religious leaders complained that the crowds were too enthusiastic, Jesus underlined the *inevitability* of His victory: "I tell you, if these become silent, the stones will cry out!" (v. 40).

Jesus then scored a dramatic touchdown when he expelled the merchants and moneychangers from the Temple (see vv. 45,46). He converted the extra point when, subsequently, He was able to teach daily in the Temple in spite of the religious leaders' hatred (see v. 47). This is very significant because the Temple was the citadel of the religious leaders. Jesus took it over and transformed the place into His pulpit.

The multitudes, so despised by the religious establishment, became His shield and made it impossible for the chief priests and scribes to even *attempt* to do harm to Jesus: "And they could not find anything that they might do, for all the people were hanging upon His words" (v. 48).

A Clear Path to Victory

In the ensuing days, Jesus' opposition vanished as His enemies were discredited and they turned tail. By then the spiritual climate had become the polar opposite of the discouraging days of chapter 9.

Jesus chose not to answer the questions of the opposition anymore (see Luke 20:1-8). The religious leaders, who once held such power over the people, became afraid of the multitudes surrounding Jesus, a fact that forced them to send spies since they dared not come near Him. The spies' mission? To get near to Jesus and catch Him in a subversive statement that would allow them to deliver Him up to the authority of the Roman governor (see v. 20).

But the spies failed and became silenced (see v. 26). Eventually, they lost their courage:

And some of the scribes answered and said, "Teacher, You have spoken well." For they did not have courage to question Him any longer about anything (Luke 20:39,40).

Jesus took total control of the situation, confidently stating, "Heaven and earth will pass away, but My words will not pass away" (Luke 21:33). As there was no significant opposition at hand, with the full backing of the multitudes Jesus took over his opponents' turf: "During the day He was teaching in the temple. . . . And all the people would get up early in the morning to come to Him in the temple to listen to Him" (vv. 37,38).

Satan Loses Control

Satan finally came into the open because his minions were powerless before the common folk who so enthusiastically and in such large numbers rallied around Jesus. You know a football team is in trouble when its overweight coach benches the quarterback, borrows his jersey and enters the field to try to execute a crucial fourth-down play. This is exactly what happened when Satan made his move to enter Judas (see Luke 22:3).

At first Judas proved to be very helpful as he knew where Jesus prayed alone at night and offered to betray Him to the chief priests (see v. 4). Satan might have said to himself, *I had it all wrong. I've been using demons, religious leaders, nature, and I got nowhere. The moment I laid my hands on one of His disciples, I was already inside Jesus' 20-yard line!* Motivated by his first taste of success in some time, Satan demanded permission to draft another player, Peter: "Simon, Simon, behold, Satan has demanded permission to sift you like wheat" (Luke 22:31).

What Satan didn't notice was that Jesus first faked to His right, then swung to His left and was set to throw a Hail Mary pass that would devastate the devil and his demonic empire. Only a few weeks later, on the Day of Pentecost, Simon Peter would kneel down, grab the handles of the gates of hell, pull them open and announce into the very pit of hell, "The first

3,000 captives in line, come on out!" When this happened, Satan could only watch in total disbelief as Peter led the first of many liberating raids against his mortally wounded kingdom.

In the meantime, Jesus would become the ultimate Lamb by surrendering Himself, choosing not to retaliate but to bless instead, all of which led to total victory in Luke 23. There He turned Satan's wolves into His lambs: He lead the thief to salvation and the centurion to faith, and the multitudes went away beating their breasts, realizing they had been party to a major mistake. This set the stage for the mass conversions that began on the Day of Pentecost.

I trust that you see in this quick survey of the Gospel of Luke two very different spiritual climates: an increasingly hostile climate in the first nine chapters and an absolutely favorable one in the final chapters.

How and When the Climate Changed

At what point in time did the spiritual climate change? It happened in Luke 10, when the same demonic powers who had buffeted Jesus and defeated several of His disciples suddenly lost the upper hand and eventually surrendered. Jesus had sent 70 of His disciples out, two by two, to proclaim the coming of the Kingdom in every city where He planned to visit:

> And the seventy returned with joy, saying, "Lord, even the demons are subject to us in Your name" (Luke 10:17).

Jesus explained the reason behind this turn of events for the better: "I was watching Satan fall from heaven like lightning" (v. 18). In other words, Satan himself had suffered a *major* defeat.

Now that we know *when* the climate changed, let us see *how* it was changed. What was it that produced this dramatic transformation? The key moment was when the Seventy, unlike the Twelve, agreed to mix in a friendly and conciliatory manner with the same people the devil was using against Jesus—"the wolves," as Jesus called them (Luke 10:3). *The change happened precisely when the disciples spoke peace over those who were poised to harm them.* This action would then lead to reconciliation and fellowship (see vv. 5,7). At that precise moment, Satan's *human* army was neutralized, and they eventually defected when the kingdom of God came near to them.

To understand how this works, it is crucial to realize that the devil cannot hurt us with just one move; instead, *he needs two moves.* Satan's first move is to cause someone to hurt us badly enough that we let the sun set on our resulting anger. When we do this, we give room to the devil (see Eph. 4:27). Then he promptly moves in, walking right into our own camp, with full capability to harm us, because *we have given him the opportunity to do so.* Our refusal to forgive constitutes a curse of sorts, as illustrated in the parable of the two debtors in Matthew 18:22-35. In this story both the offender and the offended were turned over to the torturers (the devil and his demons). Evidently, the devil knows how to deliver this one-two punch to gain jurisdiction over us. This is the bad news. Now let us hear the *good* news.

How Satan Falls

If unresolved anger gives jurisdiction to the devil, then blessing those he uses to make us angry should *void* such jurisdiction. By speaking peace over every city, the Seventy voided the jurisdiction the devil had in a vast region. Without authority on which to stand, the devil had nowhere to go but down, as reported by Jesus: "I was watching Satan fall from heaven like lightning" (Luke 10:18).

The fall of Satan was precipitated by Jesus' sending the Seventy "to every city and place where He Himself was going to come" (Luke 10:1). Jesus' move was an *enveloping* strategy designed to cover a whole area with its myriad of towns and villages and not just one or two houses. This strategy was replicat-

ed in San Nicolas on Wednesday evening of our weeklong thrust, when peace was spoken over every home in town, every sidewalk was prayer walked and every neighborhood had a canopy of prayer raised over it. By reversing the process through which the devil had obtained jurisdiction, we caused him to fall and his army to flee or capitulate. When the commanding general surrenders or flees, the privates follow suit immediately: "Lord, even the demons are subject to us" (Luke 10:17).

BY REVERSING THE PROCESS THROUGH WHICH THE DEVIL HAD OBTAINED JURISDICTION, WE CAUSED HIM TO FALL AND HIS ARMY TO FLEE OR CAPITULATE.

When we did this, blessing an entire city in one night, I sensed that something powerful had happened; but I did not understand exactly what it was, much less the extent to which it happened. It was like the first subtle change in temperature or a slight shift in the wind, small but noticeable, that precedes greater changes in the weather. That week we saw the Church in San Nicolas gain the upper hand in its struggle against the forces of evil. This was clearly in evidence for the first time on Saturday when every home in town was visited and so many came to the prayer fair. The change in climate was confirmed by the natural way in which the power of God flowed at the prayer fair prayer stations and by how readily people received the Lord.

Satan Crushed by the God of Peace

I asked the Lord why this victory over darkness looked and felt so easy, and He directed me to Romans 16:20 (emphasis added): "And the God of *peace* will soon crush Satan *under your feet*." This verse opened my eyes to a monumental mistake we had been making in spiritual warfare: *We rated war higher than peace*. It is not the God of war but the God of *peace* who crushes Satan, and He does it under *our* feet, hence the need for us to walk in peace.

Jesus has defeated the devil already. He did that at Calvary. Now we are to march on the ground where Satan lies defeated by the blood shed at the Cross; and as we walk in peace, we step on the fallen foe and God crushes his head under our feet. This is exactly what happened on Wednesday evening as we prayer walked the city of San Nicolas in peace. To put this in a wider biblical context, let us take a look at Ephesians, the book *par excellence* on city reaching.

In his letter to the Church in Ephesus, Paul does not introduce the principles of spiritual warfare against the devil and the forces of darkness *until he has first taught the Church how to make peace* in six major categories that represent divisions, or gaps, affecting groups of people in society. Paul commands us to bridge these six gaps—the ethnic gap, the denominational gap, the ministerial gap, the gender gap, the age gap and the wealth gap—*before any warfare against the devil is to be initiated*. We will take a closer look at these gaps and how to bridge them in chapter 5; but it is important that we understand Paul's prescription for city reaching: Make peace in the city before making war in the heavenlies.

This is reinforced by his preface to spiritual warfare, in which he instructs us to "be strong in the Lord *and* in the power of His might" (Eph. 6:10, *NKJV*, emphasis added). These are two different sets of instructions as indicated by the conjunction. Each phrase identifies the key component of a powerful two-part formula. The first is *defensive*; the second is *offensive*. More importantly, the latter should not be initiated until the former has been fully executed.

Don't Just Put on the Armor— Put on the Full Armor

To be strong in the Lord, in the context of the whole epistle, means the bridging of these six gaps, since in Christ there is neither Jew nor Gentile (ethnic gap), neither Paul nor Cephas nor Apollos (denominational and ministerial gaps), neither male nor female (gender gap), and both parents and children and masters and slaves (age and wealth gaps) have the same Father and Lord in heaven, in whom there is no partiality (see Rom. 10:12; 1 Cor. 3:21,22; Gal. 3:28; Eph. 6:9).

Having taken care of this most important defensive maneuver, now Paul points to the enemy and highlights the need to be strong in the power of the Lord's might to carry out the offensive dimension:

Put on the full armor of God, that you may be able to stand firm against the schemes of the devil. For our struggle is not against flesh and blood, but against the rulers, against the powers, against the world forces of this darkness, against the spiritual forces of wickedness in the heavenly places. Therefore, take up the full armor of God (Eph. 6:11-13).

It is important to notice that twice in this passage Paul indicates the need to put on the *full* armor of God. We will soon see why.

First comes *the belt of truth*. We put this on when the Holy Spirit, the Spirit of truth, convicted us of our spiritual poverty, convinced us of our sin and revealed to us the wonderful salvation available in Christ.

This is followed by the *breastplate of righteousness*, which is Christ's righteousness and refers to us appropriating it by faith in His atoning death. We put this on the day we were saved.

The third piece of armor is *key* to the subject at hand: *"having shod [our] feet with the preparation of the gospel of peace"* (Eph. 6:15). For the sake of easier visualization I will describe this as "putting on the sandals of the gospel of peace." When we put on our shoes or sandals, it's because we are about to walk. That is why we never wear shoes to bed. Therefore, the instruction to put this piece of armor on implies that we are to walk—and not just to walk, but to walk *in peace*. I submit that this is designed to see Satan crushed under our feet (see Rom. 16:20).

So how do we walk in peace? By speaking peace over those who have cursed us. This is a countermove against the devil, who used to have *us* under *his* feet. Now we are able to bring him under our feet to watch him be crushed, and we do this by removing every jurisdiction given to him through anger (see Eph. 4:26,27). This is what happened in Luke 10 when the Seventy went out to every town and village. This is also what we saw first in San Nicolas and later in scores of cities all over the world.

The fall of Satan and his removal from our immediate sphere is confirmed by the use of the next weapon, *the shield of faith*, with which "you will be able to extinguish all the flaming missiles of the evil one" (Eph. 6:16). We can categorically conclude that the devil has left the premises and is no longer nearby because of the weapon he is using at this point: missiles. Missiles are never fired at close range but always from a distance. What is the implication of this? That the devil has left the area and is reduced to firing at us from afar. When did he flee? When we walked in peace, voiding jurisdictions granted to him through anger inside our sphere of influence.

Is It Possible to Kick the Devil Out of Town?

James touches on this subject when he assures us that the devil "will flee" from us (Jas. 4:7). The anger component necessary for the devil to obtain jurisdiction over us is also identified by James when he makes reference to fights and quarrels among Christians (see Jas. 4:2). Having identified the cause-and-effect relationship between fights or quarrels and satanic proximity, James then tells us that *it is possible to remove the devil from our proximity*. I submit to you that this means it is possible to kick the devil out of town, literally.

James is not showing how one person can make the devil flee from him or her but how *a body of believers*—and, consequently, the area where they live—can be rid of him. He addresses the epistle not to an individual but "to the twelve tribes who are dispersed abroad" (Jas. 1:1). Nearly all of chapter 4 is written in the plural form. Therefore, when James says

"Resist the devil and he will flee from *you*" (Jas. 4:7, emphasis added), he means from *all of you* (plural). The implication is unavoidable: It is possible to remove the devil from our homes, our neighborhoods, our cities and our states. By removing I mean to take away from Satan the upper hand he has enjoyed for so long in the spirit world, so that the Church has the advantage instead. We have seen this happen in cities, and now we are beginning to see it take place in regions and in nations, as in the case of Singapore, the Philippines and others, as we will see later.

I submit to you that one of the greatest mistakes made in spiritual warfare literature and in practice has been to overlook the power of walking in peace—a weapon truly capable of removing the devil from our midst. What we have foolishly chosen instead is hand-to-hand combat. Any commando will tell you that hand-to-hand combat is the most dangerous way to fight a war. This is why it is crucial that we make our ultimate objective changing the spiritual climate and not just haphazardly praying for our neighbors.

Now that the concept of prayer evangelism is fast becoming mainstream and lighthouses of prayer are springing up everywhere, nothing would please the devil more than the Church failing to discover that the secret to victory resides in changing the spiritual climate over entire regions to force him to flee. It *is* possible for the Church to take control of the spiritual climate, but it requires a concerted, enveloping movement like the one described in this chapter.

If this is so, the question must be asked, Why isn't it happening? If the principle is so simple and so clear in the Scriptures, why have we missed it all these years? And why, after it has been shown to us, do we *continue* to miss it? The answer lies in a weapon the devil uses unhindered simply because *we do not have the slightest clue that he has access to it.* To learn what his secret weapon is and how the remainder of our armor comes into play, please read on.

4

The Truth About Binary Truths

*Satan has manipulated our understanding of
the Word of God to prevent acceptance of new paradigms that
will allow our cities to be transformed.*

The Church has authority "over all the power of the enemy" (Luke 10:19). This authority comes from the highest source, the Lord Himself, and it cannot be countermanded or overpowered. Since the evil one and his power are under the Church's domain, what device does he have at his disposal that enables him to keep the Church in check despite our *decisive* advantage? I submit to you that Satan manipulates our understanding of the Word of God to produce wrong paradigms. Before we look at the paradigm shifts—changes in our thinking—that this book is so much about, it is imperative that we recognize and understand the devil's strategy for keeping the Church from exercising its God-given authority over him.

I need to introduce a very shocking truth here: The devil has bewitched the Church. As blasphemous as this may sound, it is *entirely* biblical.

In the New Testament we find evidence that he is capable of this: "You foolish Galatians, who has bewitched you, before whose eyes Jesus Christ was publicly portrayed as crucified?" (Gal. 3:1). The word "bewitched" means "to have come under an evil spell," the source of which can be none other than the devil himself. In the case of the Galatians, the evil one infiltrated their thinking processes (paradigms), leading them away from the supernatural dimension of the Cross and bringing them down to the level of human speculation: "Are you so foolish? Having begun by the Spirit, are you now being perfected by the flesh?" (Gal. 3:3).

Satan accomplishes his deception of the Church in a very subtle manner. As Jack Hayford says, the devil knows better than to jump out at us from behind a bush and shout, "Turn away from God!" We're not going to fall for that.[1] Nor is he going to appear to us as a college basketball mascot, sporting horns and a tail and prodding us with a pitchfork. On the contrary, the Bible portrays the devil as one who presents himself as knowledgeable and respectable, even as he systematically aims to control the mind of his interlocutor. How does he do this? By misusing the Word of God.

The Match of the Ages

In any championship sporting event that is to be decided by a best-of-three match—meaning the winning team must win two out of three games to win the match—the decisive game is the second one. This is so because if a team has won the first game, they need only to win the second to become the champions. On the other hand, the other team desperately needs to win the second game just to "stay alive," to force the tiebreaker to be played. But if they *can* win the second game, momentum swings over to their side. The second match is *key*.

The Bible tells us about one such championship match that took place in the Palestine wilderness circa A.D. 30. On one side was Jesus, the Son of God; on the opposing side, Satan, the god of this world. This was the match of the ages. At the end of the first round, the scoreboard read, "Jesus 1, Satan 0." Going into the second round, the devil knew he had to win or *he was finished.*

When a team and its coach are in this predicament, it is imperative that they use their best play, take their best shot, in order to win that most conclusive round. In soccer, when the team that is behind desperately needs to score, the coach sends every one of his players forward, *including the goalie!* When Satan found himself in this deficit situation, what weapon did he choose? The Word of God (see Matt. 4:5,6)—the *written* Word! I submit to you that the devil uses the same tactics today, and we need to unmask his schemes.

Consider for a moment the arrogance of Satan, who chose to tempt Jesus, *the* Word, with the written Word. Even though he failed that day, the devil has not changed his tactics in 2,000 years. Satan is a schemer and a deceiver, and he tries to manipulate the Word of God in his dealings with the Church, hoping to gain a decisive and *undetected* advantage over us.

How does Satan use the Bible against us? Exactly the same way he did when he tempted Jesus. He neither altered nor misquoted the Word. Instead, his strategy had to do with suggesting an interpretation and application of the text he quoted.

Good Quote but Deceitful Application

Satan is constantly trying to produce the *opposite* effect of what the unalterable written Word is designed for. His schemes are most effective when it comes to the misapplication of what I call *binary truths*. By this I mean truths that are paralleled within the same verse or passage—for example, grace and truth in John 1:14, power and wisdom in 1 Corinthians 1:24 and mercy and grace in Luke 10:30-37.

These truths are presented in pairs because each component is designed to synergistically energize the other. There is an exponential power latent within each of these truths that is released when used in the right *proportion* and in the correct *sequence*. It is like epoxy, the liquid glue that comes in two separate tubes, the contents of which must be mixed together in equal parts to cause the chemical reaction that will produce phenomenal gluing power. If you use more of one tube than the other, the chemical reaction will not take place or will partially occur, leaving a glue that is not nearly as powerful or durable.

The Bible contains many examples of binary truths. However, there are three in particular that Satan uses in his primary efforts at deception. Why these three? Because these three sets of truths are essential to our understanding of the incarnation of God (grace and truth), the resurrection of Jesus (power and wisdom) and the work of the Holy Spirit in the unbeliever (mercy and grace). A proper understanding of these binary truths is essential if the Church is to adopt the new paradigms that will enable us to reach our cities for Christ. Let us examine these binary truths one at a time.

Grace and Truth

John 1:14 reads, "And the Word became flesh, and dwelt among us, and we beheld His glory, glory as of the only begotten from the Father, *full of grace and truth*" (emphasis added). John lists first grace and then truth to describe what he and others saw when they laid eyes on Jesus. First they saw grace and then—and only then—they saw truth. This sequence is very important. Not only are the words in the Bible inspired, but so is the order in which they are presented.

The sequence in this passage tells us that Jesus carried up front the right equipment to connect with sinners: grace. Only sinners can benefit from His grace, and only grace enables a three-times-holy God to come in contact with sinners without compromising His holiness.

All through the gospels we see Jesus comfortably welcoming sinners and being welcomed by them. With the exception of the Pharisees and the other religious leaders, no sinner ever failed to connect with Jesus. The dirtier and lower a sinner, the more he or she seemed to be attracted to Jesus. This was certainly the case with Zaccheus, perhaps the biggest crook in Palestine at the time; the woman caught by a mob in the very act of adultery; Mary Magdalene, whose life had been characterized by immorality and demonic oppression; the thief on the cross; the Samaritan woman at the well, a true untouchable whom Jesus touched; and many others. All these "certified" sinners were intensely drawn to Jesus. Why? Because when they first laid eyes on Him, what they saw was a kind of grace that told them that rejection—the biggest concern for someone immersed in sin— was not even a *possibility* with Jesus.

Sinners flocked to Him by the thousands, attracted by the grace He openly projected. In Luke 9:51-53, we learn that the Samaritans did not rally to Him because He deliberately hid His face from them. If they had seen His face, they would have been drawn to Him because His face had the word "welcome" engraved on it in letters of grace. Once sinners came to Him, He then taught them truth—divine truth, exacting and costly in the extreme but *always* palatable because of the context of grace in which it was presented.

Reversing the Order of the Components Presents a Different Jesus

Where have we gone wrong with sinners today? We have reversed the order of the components in the grace-truth binary set. When we introduce Jesus to people, we usually present Him as a truth that people must *first* understand, accept and obey as a *precondition* to receiving grace. So when we preach to sinners, we spend the bulk of our time expounding on their wickedness and on how much they deserve hell, and we devote only a tiny fragment of the time presenting grace—and this only at the very end.

We have been trained to "tell it like it is." Unfortunately, we often choose the harsh approach a prosecuting attorney would use to coerce a defendant into admitting his crime on the witness stand. However, the truth about the lost—their sinful nature, their wicked lifestyle and the awful consequences of their depraved nature—is self-evident. Sinners do not need much convincing that they are rotting from the inside out. They already know this and would hardly argue against it. What they do not want or need is Christians telling them so, especially when we do it with a holier-than-thou attitude.

If Jesus had focused on that painful dimension as an opener, an ice breaker, during his earthly ministry, people would have felt immediately rejected. This is why He first showed Himself full of grace. Grace is the perfect remedy for the sin people find themselves wallowing in. The Lord's grace, then and now, projects the irresistible message that He is *willing* and *eager* to accept us the way we are. Grace conveys the distinct impression that we have nothing to lose and *everything* to gain. Afterwards, once we are secure in His loving embrace, He spoon-feeds us truth in order to gradually transform us and to conform us to His image.

A Loving Hug Before a Much-Needed Bath

GRACE CONVEYS THE DISTINCT IMPRESSION THAT SINNERS HAVE NOTHING TO LOSE AND EVERYTHING TO GAIN BY COMING TO CHRIST.

Throughout the gospels Jesus reached out to sinners, telling parables that highlighted the gracious nature of God incarnate. In the parable of the prodigal son, the righteous father caught sight of a young man who looked like his son but was covered with pig slop. His returning son looked and smelled like a pig, dressed in rags and totally deprived of the most elemental trace of dignity. Did he wait for his son to repent, kneel down and beg to be welcomed back? No! The father, who had long been waiting and watching for his son, saw the young man first, ran toward him, embraced him, kissed him and ordered that he be adorned in clothing that reflected sonship rather than servanthood. The father did all this while the son was still in shameful rags! By telling this parable Jesus left no doubt of where He stood on the issue of grace first.

Unfortunately, by reversing the order of the elements (grace and truth) we tragically diminish their effectiveness. People do not feel attracted to *our* Jesus because before we talk about His love and compassion for sinners, we tend to emphasize His hatred of sin and the penalty unrepentant sinners must pay. And we do this with so much intensity that sinners have no option but to feel rejected. We need to learn from Jesus, who is "gentle and humble in heart" (Matt. 11:29).

He was born into a sinful world that was at total enmity with God. He lived 33 years in a spiritual atmosphere horribly polluted by man's sinfulness. He knew about man's depravity and He endured it because His eyes were set on the Cross and on the shedding of His redemptive blood for those held in spiritual chains. Jesus, the Holy One, is no stranger to the presence of sin. This is why He is full of grace.

Aspiring Maradona Gets in Trouble

I learned the difference between *grace and truth* and *truth and grace* as a soccer-minded boy growing up in Argentina. My father was a strict disciplinarian. He was fair but also immovable when it came to passing sentence and administering the corresponding physical punishment when we were found guilty of violating rules explained to us beforehand. One of those rules was not to play soccer inside the house, especially not in our beautiful indoor patio on the second floor, which was enclosed by stained-glass windows. The reason was obvious: Soccer balls and stained-glass windows do not mix.

I had no problem with this rule as it seemed both logical and necessary. And I faithfully obeyed it . . . until the day I came out of my bedroom and saw a soccer ball positioned like a seductress at the very center of the indoor patio. At that moment I understood what Eve must have felt when she first laid eyes on the forbidden fruit. I tried to resist the temptation, but that ball was too enticing, too alluring, too overpowering! Every Argentine boy is born with a soccer ball next to his diaper bag; and every father, uncle and grandpa tells him that he will be the next Maradona.[2] Thus the temptation to play with that ball was almost impossible for me to resist!

At first I was very cautious and careful. I began by touching the ball with the tip of my shoe. I gently balanced it on my foot and landed it on my knee. From there it went to my right shoulder, bounced on the top of my head and over to my left shoulder from where I dropped it in the right place and at the right moment for my swinging left foot to connect in mid-air. It felt so good!

Inebriated by this feeling, I kicked the ball *carefully* against the wall. I could not help but experience delight as I saw the ball sprightly bouncing back toward me. After a while I found myself enjoying the back-and-forth rhythmic dialogue with the wall. Once I kicked the ball a bit too high and it hit a window, but I was relieved when nothing bad happened. *Maybe those windows are shatterproof after all,* a quiet voice whispered in my subconscious. *Wouldn't that be wonderful?* I said to myself.

Deceived and lulled into a false sense of security, I increased the tempo and force of each kick as the ball bounced all over the patio. I pictured myself playing in the final match of the World Cup. Argentina was the finalist against archrival England, and I was wearing the Argentine blue-and-white jersey with the number 10 emblazoned on the front and back. The score was tied, and only one minute remained on the clock. A corner kick was awarded to Argentina and as the ball zoomed toward me I swung around and in midstride kicked it with all my might. The ball overpowered the goalie and made it into the net. *Goal! Goal! Argentine goal!*

But instead of the roaring crowd and the battery of radio announcers shouting my name, I heard the distinct sound of shattered glass falling to the floor. Reality painfully dawned on me: I was not playing in the final match of the World Cup but in the indoor patio of our house. *I had just destroyed a stained glass window!* I had disobeyed my father, and the consequences of my disobedience lay all over the floor in the form of colorful, glassy debris.

The Day I Left Home . . . at Age Seven!

The truth sank in, and I was frightened. My father had warned me in no uncertain terms about the consequences of disobeying his command. I did not want to face him. He was at work and not due to return for a couple of hours, but I was already overwhelmed by fear. I knew what was coming, and I did not want to face it. So that day I left home, at age seven, with the intention of never returning.

I hurriedly packed my few belongings, including my pet cricket. I pocketed some crackers and left. I decided to camp near the Catholic church for the night. I guess that, subconsciously, I wanted to be near God in case my dad showed up!

I stayed there for hours. At about 10 P.M., my mother finally found me. She said, "Come, let us go home."

I said, "Never. Dad will kill me. I know what is coming to me."

Then she spoke the most reassuring words: "I have talked to your father, and he has agreed to forgive you. He still wants to talk to you; but he will not punish you. He has decided to be gracious—at my request, of course."

That was good news! I did not care whose request it was as long as he was going to be gracious. I immediately agreed to go home with my mother. I knew I had to face my father, but I was no longer running from him. In fact, I was looking forward to seeing him. Truth, when preceded by grace, is intriguing, even attractive.

Tension Between Acceptance and Approval

Reversing the biblical order in the grace-truth equation plays havoc with the central message of the gospel and with prayer evangelism in particular, especially when it comes to the natural tension between acceptance and approval. We are often reluctant to pray for the felt needs of sinners for fear that they may interpret our actions as tacit approval of their sinful behaviors. So what do we do instead? Rather than empathizing and interceding for their needs, we feel compelled to tell them *in no uncertain terms* everything that is wrong with them.

Our actions originate out of a genuine desire not to compromise the gospel; but our judgmental attitudes and lack of sympathy for the plight in which sinners find themselves comes across as rejection. This is how we end up violating the very nature of the gospel, which is supposed to be good news for sinners.

Sinners need to see that our God is indeed a God of compassion. To help them see this, we ourselves need to understand that, although Jesus is truth, that truth must be seen through the inviting prism of grace.

We Must Lift Up the Right Jesus

In another case of spiritual paralysis caused by Satan's manipulation of this binary truth, Christians often will not pray for the felt needs of the unsaved—health, work, prosperity, etc.—unless they first become Christians. If the unbeliever's business goes bankrupt, we rejoice at their demise, hoping that such failure will cause them to come to Christ. We look at the misery they find themselves in and say to ourselves, *They should have known better.* Should they have? We forget the fact that sin is a blinding condition that eventually perverts the mind, causing sinners to become spiritually insane and self-destructive.

We think, *They are old enough to know better.* Are they? Those who crucified Christ were religious leaders with a thorough knowledge of the Scriptures, and yet Christ absolved them, saying, "Father, forgive them; for they do not know what they are doing" (Luke 23:34).

Truth without grace kills. So often when we look at the lost, we focus on their sinfulness and its manifestation through destructive behavior, and we fail to draw from our God-given deposit of faith to pray for what God has in store for them. Instead of praying the promise—God's promise—we end up praying the problem—the problem that Satan created to hurt them, just as I used to do until God rebuked me.

We must confess that *everything* the devil has intended for evil, God will use for good, and that *nothing* is impossible for Him. As we do this, faith will rise and we will soon find ourselves seeing and touching things hoped for.

Let us pray the promise instead of the problem! Otherwise, we present a Jesus who blends well with our theology but is foreign to the Gospels—a Jesus whom we work hard to lift up but who fails to attract anyone, much less *everyone*, to Himself as He promised He would. Why? Because the evil one has manipulated our understanding of the Scriptures, and we end up lifting up the wrong Jesus.

Power and Wisdom

Another key binary truth is one that combines power and wisdom as described by Paul in a letter to the Corinthians. He wrote, "I determined to know nothing among you except Jesus Christ, and Him crucified" (1 Cor. 2:2). Paul is stating here in chapter 2 that *the most important* thing he taught the Corinthians was Christ crucified. What did he mean by this? Earlier, Paul had explained that Christ crucified is *first* the power of God and *then* the wisdom of God (see 1 Cor. 1:23,24). Here we see another binary truth and, as such, the order in which the components are presented is crucial. Please note that the biblical order is *first* power and *then* wisdom.

What has the enemy done with this truth? As in the case of grace and truth, the order has been reversed in much of the Church. As a result we preach a gospel that purports to present the wisdom of God, assuming that once such wisdom is received the recipient will experience the power of God. Is this necessarily wrong? No, but it is not excellent either because *it does not reflect the primary intent* of the passage, which is to say that a manifestation of the power of God leads people to God.

When we witness to a stranger, do we try to do something to help that person to *experience* the power of God so that he or she will desire to know more about His wisdom? Quite the contrary! We flood our target with all kinds of information and try to get the person to accept it as God's wisdom, and we proffer a decision to receive Christ as a preamble to experiencing His power. But that is not what Paul said to the Corinthians. He stated unequivocally that the manifestation of power must *precede* the dispensation of wisdom. This is the heart of prayer evangelism.

WE CANNOT TEACH UNBELIEVERS ABOUT JESUS WHILE SATAN IS BLINDING THEM. WE NEED TO SET THEM FREE FIRST.

We Can't Teach Captives—We Must Liberate Them First

Why is it important for sinners to experience the power of God? At least three reasons come to mind:

First, sinners are captives in Satan's dominion, and only a power encounter can set them free (see Acts 26:18). We cannot teach unbelievers about Jesus while Satan is blinding them. We need to set them free first.

Second, when unexpected, undeserved and much-needed good happens to the lost, they then become interested in knowing the identity of their benefactor. Once, someone paid our bill at a cafeteria. When we asked for the bill, the waiter told us it was already taken care of. Naturally, Ruth and I asked the waitress who our benefactor was. When somebody does something nice for you, you want to know who this person is. This is even more true when lost people experience the power of God in the form of an answer to prayer.

Third, and most important, sinners should experience the power of God *because the Bible shows this is the way it ought to be.* The Scriptures are replete with examples where God revealed Himself to people through His power. The lives of Abraham, Moses, Daniel and Joseph are dotted with example after example of the power of God opening doors to His wisdom. As a result, entire nations turned to God and multitudes of captives sought God and His truth.

Talk Is Cheap—Let Deeds Prove Your Words

Elijah faced the prophets of Baal on Mount Carmel at a time when the entire nation was under the power of evil. Israel was ruled by an evil king, a bad situation significantly compounded by the machinations of the king's treacherous wife, Jezebel. Conditions could not have been worse. How did Elijah handle it? Not very well at first:

> And Elijah came near to all the people and said, "How long will you hesitate between two opinions? If the LORD is God, follow Him; but if Baal, follow him." But the people did not answer him a word (1 Kings 18:21).

Elijah stated the truth in the abstract. Consequently, the people's reaction couldn't have been more passive.

However, when Elijah moved on to the level of a power encounter, he got the response he was looking for. When he proposed, "I will build an altar to my God, and you build one to your god, and the god who answers by fire, let him be God," the people replied, "Now that's a good idea!" (see 1 Kings 18:24). While Elijah was just preaching, nothing happened. Talk is cheap. The moment he proposed a power encounter, he was able to engage the people. That very day God's power was publicly displayed in answer to prayer, and the nation turned to God.

Power must precede wisdom. By this I do not mean that we should not preach the wisdom found in the Word of God or that we should not teach God's counsel. I am all for that. However, when it comes to setting the captives free, a power encounter is required. Such an encounter must be generated by the bold proclamation of the Word of God and not a collection of bland phrases. It must be so bold as to allow—*to require*, if you may—God to intervene by confirming the word with the signs that follow (see Mark 16:20).

Same-Day Baptisms

In the book of Acts, new converts were baptized the moment they believed in Jesus; it follows that we should do the same today. But we don't. Instead, we consider it unwise to baptize a person immediately after his or her conversion. We deign that extensive and intensive teaching must take place first. In fact, this is a prerequisite in the majority of churches today.

Why do we not baptize people right after conversion? Because they are not ready, we say—first they need to be taught (wisdom) so that they may experience the fullness of Christ (power). The problem with this approach, which appears so right and righteous on the surface, is that quite often it does not work. In fact, it may produce the opposite of the intended results. Let me explain.

Do It Right Now or It Will Do You in Later

We tell sinners that all they need to do to be saved is to receive Jesus into their hearts. When they agree, we walk them through a brief sinner's prayer, after which we assure them that they are now Christians.

Do we baptize them right away? Almost never! Why not? They lack teaching (wisdom), so we put them through a long new members' baptismal class. When they graduate, we finally baptize them on the assumption that they now have enough wisdom to be able to experience the power of God. The problem is that after they emerge from the baptismal waters, they hardly pray, they do not tithe, they do not witness, they still watch pornographic movies and, worst of all, they move through the ranks and become elders—and drive us nuts!

Why is this approach so ineffective? Because although these new believers now understand human doctrines and have a semblance of piety, they deny the effectiveness of the gospel because they have not experienced divine power (see 2 Tim. 3:5). Paul's teaching to the Corinthians was "not in persuasive words of wisdom, but in demonstration of the Spirit and of power, that [their] faith should not rest on the wisdom of men, but on the power of God" (1 Cor. 2:4,5). The faith of many converts is based on the wisdom of men rather than on the power of God because they came into the Kingdom through an intellectual argument rather than through a power encounter.

Even though the proper elements (wisdom and power) are present in our formula, by altering the God-decreed sequence, we end up with the wrong results. Whether you're baking a cake or harnessing the energy of a nuclear reaction, mixing the right ingredients is not enough; you must also use them in the right order. If you want to enjoy a satisfying horseback ride, three elements are required: a horse, a rider (you) and knowing which one of the two goes on top! Otherwise, you may have a most frustrating experience carrying the horse on your back.

Mercy and Grace

Perhaps the area where the violation of binary truths has caused the greatest damage to the cause of evangelism is the one affecting the interaction between mercy and grace.

God has provided us with mercy and grace as reciprocally complementary tools for reaching out to the lost. Mercy is a benevolent act by which people do not get what they deserve. Grace is a divine impartation by which they do get what they do not deserve. Mercy and grace are designed to be used in tandem. The Scriptures portray God as both merciful *and* gracious. The same is true of Jesus.

Unfortunately, the Church has exalted grace at the expense of mercy; we are rich in the proclamation of grace but extremely poor in the demonstration of mercy.

Grace, in order to be of help to sinners, requires their acknowledgment and repentance of sin. So in our message we emphasize their sinfulness in an attempt to help them see the devastating eternal consequences of sin. But this approach—grace presented in a context devoid of mercy—projects rejection and, more often than not, sinners walk away angry and feeling forsaken.

And those who do receive the Lord are told, "Everything has been forgiven . . . 2,000 years ago!" First, we make them feel the ugliness of their sin, and when they repent, we tell them, "Oh, don't worry, it is all forgiven." It sounds like a bad joke. Why don't we begin with a clear pronouncement that all their sins were forgiven when Christ died on the cross? Many preachers would see this as cheapening the gospel. Grace is anything but cheap—to receive it, sinners must pay the highest price: total surrender to Jesus. Remember, the gospel is *good* news, and what better news to announce to a lost world than all their sins have been forgiven?

The Vertical Dimension Cannot Stand Without the Horizontal

In Luke 10, a lawyer asked Jesus what he should do to inherit eternal life. Jesus asked him what he understood the Scriptures to say on this matter:

> And He said to him, "What is written in the Law? How does it read to you?"
>
> And he answered and said, "YOU SHALL LOVE THE LORD YOUR GOD WITH ALL YOUR HEART, AND WITH ALL YOUR SOUL, AND WITH ALL YOUR STRENGTH, AND WITH ALL YOUR MIND; AND YOUR NEIGHBOR AS YOURSELF."
>
> And [Jesus] said to him, "You have answered correctly; DO THIS, AND YOU WILL LIVE" (Luke 10:26-28).

Notice that Jesus moved immediately from the vertical dimension of faith—the man's love for God—to the horizontal dimension—his love for his neighbor.

When Jesus challenged him to do something radical to prove that he loved his neighbor, the lawyer became defensive: "And who is my neighbor?" (v. 29). In answer, Jesus told the parable of the good Samaritan. At the end of the story, He asked the question, "[Who] do you think proved to be a neighbor to the man who fell into the robbers' hands?" (v. 36). The lawyer answered correctly, "The one who showed mercy" (v. 37).

In the story, the man who fell among thieves and his rescuer were social adversaries, one being Jewish and the other Samaritan. The lesson here is clear: Do not give your adversary what he deserves but, rather, what he does *not* deserve. In the parable this meant giving him care, medicine, food and shelter even though he neither deserved nor expected it, since Jews and Samaritans were to have no dealings with one another.

By causing us to concentrate almost exclusively on the message of grace at the expense of mercy, the devil has lured us into preaching a gospel that is not good news at all and, consequently, very few people wish to hear it. Grace is most effective when it is preceded by a tangible demonstration of mercy. When our attitude is, *I choose not to give to you what you deserve but, rather, I choose to minister to your felt needs,* then we create an atmosphere of total, unconditional acceptance.

On the other hand, when we preach grace devoid of tangible expressions of mercy, our message fails, because grace can only be activated by a voluntary confession of sin on the part of the sinner. Who would want to confess their sins when there is no forthright promise of forgiveness? This is like a gang of criminals trapped in a building surrounded by the police, and the police announce over loudspeakers, "We are taking no prisoners. Anyone who comes out will be shot on sight. Now, please, come out with your hands up." Who among the criminals would dare comply? Only someone who is certifiably insane!

This is exactly the way sinners feel when there is no tangible expression of mercy framing our proclamation of grace. The vertical dimension of grace cannot stand without the horizontal dimension of mercy.

Mercy Is the Forerunner of Grace

At the prayer fairs mentioned earlier, we prayed for many people who we knew or sensed were living in sin. However, we chose to be merciful by not giving to them what they deserved—judgment, punishment, rejection—but instead ministering to them. In case after case, sinners who were touched by God in response to our prayers immediately confessed their sins. They said things like, "I do not understand it. Why would God bless me like this when I have been insulting Him?" or "We are amazed that God will answer your prayers on our behalf when my girlfriend and I are living in sin. Why would God do something like that?" These kinds of questions were triggered by an act of *mercy* on our part, which always opens the door to the proclamation of the *grace* of God.

We Must Pull Down Satanic Strongholds in Our Minds

It is important that we realize the devil is using the Word of God to deceive us, especially by reversing the sequence or altering the proportion of the components presented in these biblical binary truths. This is why the new paradigms presented in the next few chapters have taken so long to become established in the Church.

We must take to heart Paul's teaching on spiritual strongholds in 2 Corinthians 10:3-5. There he makes it crystal clear that we must knock down the lofty partitions in our minds that allow us to speculate on the one hand while subscribing to the Word of God on the other. Furthermore, he exhorts us to take every thought—not just the evil ones, but *all* of them—captive to the obedience of Christ. This subject is so vital that I dedicated an entire chapter to it in *That None Should Perish*.[3]

When we look further at Paul's reference to the spiritual bewitchment of the churches in the province of Galatia (see Gal. 3:1), it is interesting to note that his statement comes right after one of the best known verses in the New Testament:

> I have been crucified with Christ; and it is no longer I who live, but Christ lives in me; and the life which I now live in the flesh I live by faith in the Son of God, who loved me, and delivered Himself up for me (Gal 2:20).

In this context, the ensuing verses indicate that when we operate in our own flesh, outside of Christ—that is, in the natural as opposed to the supernatural—we become vulnerable to the schemes of the evil one. At no time is this approach more lethal than when we foolishly label our natural speculations as divine wisdom, and we overlook the need to experience God's power as a precondition to understanding His supernatural wisdom.

When Jesus said, "You shall know the truth, and the truth shall make you free" (John 8:32), He was not talking about acknowledging a set of facts in our minds. Knowing the truth means *experiencing* the truth through a power encounter rather than the inconsequential intellectual assent we have made it out to be in the Western Church. When God's truth invades the *soul*, it tears down Satan's strongholds, breaks the chain of sinful habits and opens the eyes to the good news of the gospel. Such a power encounter leaves one with an unquenchable thirst for His wisdom.

Watch Out for Satan's Last Shot!

We are involved in a spiritual struggle to the finish against Satan and his forces of wickedness for the souls of men and women.

But to emerge victorious from this struggle, we must put on the *full* armor of God (see Eph. 6:11). It is not enough to wear *most* of the armor. And, as we saw in the previous chapter, we must also put it on in the correct sequential order. First comes the belt of truth. Second, we put on the breastplate of righteousness. Next, we slip on the sandals of the gospel of peace in order to walk in peace to destroy Satan's jurisdictions. The fourth component, the shield of faith, is designed to extinguish the fiery darts of the devil, who now has been forced to fight from a distance.

At this point the fight seems to be won, since we have been illuminated by the truth of God, clothed in His righteousness, crushed Satan under our feet and reduced him to lobbing fiery darts from a distance. For all practical purposes the devil has lost, *unless* he can move the fight to a new level.

The new battleground is where we fight for the salvation of those still in darkness. This is the threshold where Satan makes his last stand, and he will do everything in his power to bewitch the Church to prevent us from looting his camp. Please, pay close attention because this is the last spiritual frontier in the struggle for our cities. This is Satan's last shot.

Point the Sword in the Right Direction

The next piece of armor is the *helmet of salvation*. Traditionally, we have interpreted this to refer to our own salvation. This is not the case. We were saved earlier, when we put on the breastplate of righteousness. The helmet of salvation has to mean the salvation of others, namely those who are still in darkness. The helmet's high placement—on the believer's head—is for the lost to see and to know that it is available to them. The helmet assures our neighbors that they have nothing to fear, because Satan has been crushed under our feet which are shod with the sandals of the gospel of peace.

Finally, we take up *the sword of the Spirit*—the Word of God. Now the strategic role of the helmet of salvation becomes clearer. If these two pieces of the armor are misunderstood or misused, we will play right into the hands of the devil, allowing him to overrun our position and to destroy our lines. Read this carefully.

We must put on the helmet of salvation *before* the sword of the Spirit because the helmet provides direction and focus in the use of the sword (the Word). Wearing the helmet of salvation on our heads—facing *forward*, as all helmets are meant to do—provides the direction in which we are to point the sword so that it may be used for the benefit of the lost. After we have addressed the felt needs of our neighbors, we then can address their need for salvation by sharing the good news as found in the Word of God. We then point the sword in the direction of our neighbors in order to present to them Jesus as full of grace, His crucifixion as all-powerful and His message as clothed in tangible mercy.

However, when we fail to take the Word out into the city in the direction of the lost, we end up pointing the sword in one direction only—toward the Church. This is exactly what Satan is hoping for, that we will use the Word for the edification of the saints at the expense of the evangelization of the lost.

I am not saying that the Word of God should not be used for the instruction, exhortation and edification of the saints. That is a legitimate and much needed use of the Word. However, the sword of the Spirit is not meant to remain sheathed, as though its sole purpose is decorative. The Word is a powerful weapon that, when wielded, first leads us to salvation, then to personal edification and finally to salvation again—the salvation of those to whom we are to take the Word.

We see this dynamic played out in the book of Ephesians. From the first chapter through the beginning of chapter 6, Paul uses the Word of God to show how to become strong in the Lord, the first step of which is accepting the salvation offered in Christ. Once we have become strong in the Lord, Paul exhorts us to become "strong in the power of His might" (Eph. 6:10, *NKJV*) so that we will be victorious in our struggle against the devil and his minions (see v. 12). Why must we engage Satan's forces in a spiritual struggle if we are already saved, have been sanctified and are protected by His Spirit? It is not for mere personal benefit that we should take up the armor of God and do battle. We do it to loot the enemy's camp and to set the captives free.

Throughout the first five chapters of Ephesians, we see the Word of God being used to build up the Body of Christ. This is its *defensive* use. In Ephesians 6:10-17, we are directed to engage the enemy—the *offensive* use of the Word. Here the focus switches to the salvation of the lost, when the sword of the Spirit must be pointed in their direction. If we go on the offensive but point the sword in the wrong direction, we can easily wound our own Body. This happens far too often, especially when pseudo Bible experts use the Word of God to purposely and passionately inflict injuries on saints with whom they disagree. Hours and hours of radio time and millions of dollars are wasted in this futile, self-serving and harmful exercise, while billions of people are perishing without Christ.

WE FOOLISHLY BEAUTIFY OUR TRENCHES AND REPAINT THE REVIEW GROUNDS, WHEN THERE ARE MILLIONS OF CAPTIVES WAITING TO BE FREED OVER THE NEXT HILL.

Even though the vast majority of our Bible teaching is done in a gracious manner, 99 percent of the time we use the sword of the Spirit to protect the saved, and we make very little use of it, if any, to reach the lost. This is why the Church has not yet fulfilled the Great Commission. We have secured our position in Christ; but instead of charging against the devil's strongholds with boldness, as we are commanded in Ephesians 6:19,20, we are facing the wrong direction. We foolishly beautify our trenches and repaint the review grounds for the saints to enjoy one more parade, when there are millions of captives waiting to be freed over the next hill. The sword of the Spirit is in our hands, but we are facing only one way. We must turn around and use it to attack the adversary who blinds the lost to the gospel.

Let's face it, the devil has deceived us, especially when it comes to our understanding of binary biblical truths like the ones discussed here. Our disproportionate emphasis on wisdom has preempted the power dimension of our faith, and if one thing is needed to overrun the enemy's position, it is power. And whatever power we have we are using for our own benefit rather than for the benefit of the lost. In so doing we have succumbed to the temptation that Jesus so aptly overcame when He refused to use *divine* power for *personal* comfort. It is time that we let the helmet of salvation point us in the right direction.

Let Us Pray for the Lord to Change Us, So We Can Change the World

We are about to move into a discussion of paradigm shifts that are now taking place or will take place in the worldwide Church. This is a crucial section because this is where the hope for our cities lies. We need to understand that these new paradigms have taken so long to come to the forefront because the Church has been deceived by the enemy, not by being lured into gross sin but by allowing our minds to be infiltrated and neutralized with enough *good* to quench our thirst for *excellence*, God's excellence. We need to empty ourselves before God and to be filled anew by Him before we can proceed any further. Would you join me now in praying this prayer?

O God, illuminate my mind. For You to be able to reach every aspect of it, I now take all my thoughts captive to the obedience of Christ, especially those that appeal to me because they represent deeply held theological reflections. Some of them are good; some of them may be evil. But none of them is excellent since excellence comes only from You. Please, deliver me from intellectual strongholds built with bricks baked in the oven of human traditions and cemented with fleshly pride.

O God, I surrender all to You. Help me to see the Scriptures as You see them. Help me to apply them as Jesus did. Help me to understand them as the Spirit does. Help me to use the Scriptures as You desire me to. Above all else, help me to know at all times that You came to save the lost, to set the captives free, to deliver those oppressed by the devil, and that this task is still unfinished! Help me to see that the gospel without its redemptive mission is sterile and that Bible teaching without passion for the lost is a self-serving parade on safe grounds.

Help me, O God, to understand the true magnitude of what the blood of Jesus accomplished, not just for the Church, but especially for those still held in spiritual prisons. Help me to see that You rate obedience higher than scholarship and that I must devote my life to applying the blood to the lost rather than just teaching about it to the saved.

Help me, O God, to speak the word of my testimony boldly, that in the opening of my mouth I will speak as I ought to speak— that I will fear no one but You and that I will boldly proclaim the good news to the lost over the lies and the threats of the devil. Help me to see that You are more pleased with a soldier charging ahead, even if all he has is a toothpick in his hands, than with a general with ten divisions at his disposal who is looking forward to retirement.

Help me, O God, to despise my life even unto death. Give me the courage to die for You, if that is what You call me to; but also give me the courage to die daily to my theological presuppositions, to my castles of speculation and to my citadel of humanistic introspection. Help me to see that without You, I am nothing. Help me to despise my life to the point that I will be not only ready but also eager to die for the lost, and so qualify as a good shepherd because of my willingness to lay down my life for those under my care.

O God, reprogram my mind. Pull down the strongholds that have allowed the evil one to control me and millions of Your children. Help me to see that I must move and keep on moving into the enemy's territory. Help me to hold high the helmet of salvation so that, as Satan and his demons retreat, the captives will see that we are not their enemies, as the evil one has told them, but that we are the ones who bring good news over the mountains. And, as such, make our feet blessed. Help us to move into Satan's territory so that our feet will crush his head. Yes, Lord, we know that You, the God of peace, will soon crush Satan under our feet!

O God, help me to understand the components to victory described in Revelations 12:11. Open my eyes to see that the beneficiary of the blood of the Lamb is the world, the whole world and not just those who are already safe inside the fold; that because of that precious blood and how it changed us, the devil fears the word of our testimony most of all. Help me to speak that word as Jesus would like me to speak it: boldly, fearlessly, passionately.

And finally, help me to see myself as a soldier, fearlessly charging into dangerous enemy territory, rather than as a self-appointed general, leading parades on safe grounds. Yes, Lord, help me to despise my life even unto death so that I will speak as I ought to speak for Your Kingdom to come near to those who need it the most: the lost!

Help me O God, not to be afraid on the way up of shedding tears which water the seeds in my hands, knowing that those tears will help them turn into sheaves on the way down.

I pray this in the glorious name of Jesus Christ. Amen.

Notes

1. Jack Hayford, *Resisting the Devil* (Van Nuys, CA: Soundword Tape Ministry, 1988). Audiotapes of sermons presented at The Church On The Way in November 1988.
2. Maradona was the greatest soccer player of the 1980s and a sports hero to millions.
3. See my chapter 4, "Strongholds: What They Are and How to Pull Them Down," in *That None Should Perish* (Ventura, CA: Regal Books, 1995), pp. 147-175.

5

ESTABLISHED PARADIGMS IN THE CHURCH

If you have an ear, hear what the Spirit is saying to the churches:
Be My witness in your Jerusalem first.

I have identified 17 paradigm shifts that affect the Church and its relationship with the lost in our cities. They fall into four categories: established, recent, emerging and future paradigms. I have organized them into four groups and assigned a chapter to each group.

As we have discussed, a paradigm is a conceptual grid through which reality is perceived. After studying my list, some may feel inclined to argue that only one paradigm has shifted and that my list does not constitute paradigm shifts per se, but are the side-effects of only one major paradigm shift. If that is what the reader prefers, I would like to identify that one new paradigm as the need to fulfill the Great Commission in our generation.

This particular chapter deals with four established paradigms which are recent but more senior to those discussed in the coming chapters. They are also foundational to the emergence of the others.

Paradigm #1:
One Church in the City

The concept that there are many congregations in the city but only one Church is rapidly gaining acceptance. This was not the case before the 1990s—the days when eloquent speakers drew huge national followings by using their understanding of the Scriptures to point out what was wrong with other groups, why they should be avoided and why many of them were considered unchristian—all because of what the majority of the Church today recognizes are minor differences.

As recent as a dozen years ago, even minor doctrinal were seen as malignant growths to be extirpated immediately, no matter the cost. If the cost was disunity in the Church, so be it. Today, only a few self-appointed spiritual vigilantes still make names for themselves by pointing fingers and exposing so-called heretics, as though operating a doctrinal KGB. Fading fast are the days of angry disputes and divisions being framed in the purple trappings of pure doctrine.

Calls for uniformity are giving way to calls for unity, as the concept of one Church made up of many different congregations is gaining widespread acceptance.

Tribes Blessing Tribes

During the week-long prayer evangelism thrust in my hometown of San Nicolas, the local pastors gathered for an event that was crucial to the success of our efforts there. Three pastors representing the three oldest congregations in the city, the congregations who originally brought the gospel to San Nicolas, were asked to step forward and stand facing the others. We told the rest, "Those of you who are not part of one of the groups represented here have either split from one of these congregations or came into town despising them. That is not right. Let us deal with it now."

Dramatically and spontaneously, every other pastor came forward, held hands and formed a circle. Together they prayed a corporate prayer confessing that there is only one Church in the city of San Nicolas and that every lofty thing raised against that truth must come down. Then, one by one, the pastors began to bless one another and each other's ministries. This was especially poignant and powerful for those congregations between whom wrath and anger had existed.

For the next hour or so, we heard things like, "The tribe of the Assemblies of God blesses the Christian Community tribe" and "The Baptist tribe blesses the Evangelical Union tribe." The use of the word "tribe" was consistent with the notion that the Church, like the people of Israel, consists of many tribes who together constitute one nation. That evening, when our message on holiness was broadcast via radio, the Church in the city, through its pastors, had already cleansed its hands.

Jesus in San Francisco

A new atmosphere is also beginning to take shape in the San Francisco Bay Area. In March 1996, John Isaacs, Michael Griffiths and I visited seven cities around the Bay to take stock of the spiritual environment.[1] To our surprise, we were received by a unified group of pastors in each of the seven cities. These pastors regularly prayed together and fervently hoped to see their cities reached for Christ. This is most extraordinary when one considers the history of spiritual bleakness in San Francisco and the Bay Area communities.

Sensing fertile ground, we encouraged these groups to join hands for a Bay Area-wide celebration of unity during the coming National Day of Prayer. Representatives from these groups quickly came together. A Christian radio station offered free advertising time, and a marvelous strategy was soon developed.

On the appointed day, the Church in the Bay Area—as it has chosen to call itself now—gathered in nine locations around the bay at exactly 7:00 P.M., bringing together thousands of believers. After praise and worship, pastors at each of the sites were commissioned to go to the next city. They then boarded buses, and each group "prayer rode" to the meeting in the next town. While in transit, these pastors spoke peace over cars on the freeway and over buildings along the side of the road. When they arrived at the next meeting place, each group was warmly welcomed and asked to join the ongoing intercession. At 8:45 P.M., all nine sites, linked by radio, took communion and closed with a corporate prayer blessing the Bay Area.

Earlier that day, 16 airplanes loaded with intercessors "prayer flew" over the entire Bay Area, while below them young people riding public transportation and Christians on motorcycles circled the bay, creating a ring of prayer 240 miles long![2]

Today, in the nine counties that border the San Francisco Bay, the Church has established Pray The Bay, an association of pastors dedicated to reaching the Bay Area for Christ. The association facilitates an annual prayer summit for pastors, and in 1997 it hosted the San Francisco/Oakland/San Jose crusade of Billy Graham, whose organization has rated this pastors' association as one of the best, especially in the area of prayer.

What are the odds of something so fantastic springing up in the San Francisco Bay Area, a place with a long-time reputation as the gates of hell? In human terms, nil. So how did it come together in such a quick, unexpected and extraordinary way? Because the seeds for the paradigm of one Church in the city were already germinating in the ground. The prophetic acts described above simply caused them to sprout into the open.

Interdependence Day

Paul wrote to the Corinthians, "[You do] not judge the body [of Christ] rightly. For this reason many among you are weak and sick, and a number sleep" (1 Cor. 11:29,30). When we fail to discern the true nature of the Body of Christ—many congregations, one Church—we are subject to weakness that produces sickness that leads to death. Weakness, illness and premature death are the marks of type-A people, those who see themselves as self-contained and self-sufficient.

God did not give all His gifts to one person or one congregation in the city but distributed them all over the Church. This way its members would be required to interact and be interdependent in order to be effective.

Failure to receive. God has distributed His gifts among members of the Church who meet in different congregations and many of them are culturally and theologically distant from each other. Such distance is man-made, not God-made. God's design is for the Body to grow together:

> Speaking the truth in love, we are to grow up in all aspects into Him, who is the head, even Christ, from whom *the whole body*, being fitted and held *together* by that which every joint supplies, according to the proper

working of each individual part, causes the growth of
the body for the building up of itself in love (Eph.
4:15,16, emphasis added).

Each joint, each member of the Body supplies something that
the others need. When a congregation fails to discern its part in
this operation, it will try to produce internally what God has
already provided externally through another congregation.
Through natural means (its own strength), the deluded congregation will attempt to generate a gift or ministry that God did
not equip them for in the supernatural. This working in the
flesh produces excessive wear and tear that eventually leads to
weakness and illness in the Body. God wants us to receive
through other congregations the gifts our congregations lack.

Some congregations have an evangelistic gifting, while others are gifted for teaching or mercy. In Resistencia, Argentina, it
was so refreshing when the conservatives asked the Pentecostals
to teach on the Holy Spirit, and the Pentecostals reciprocated by
asking the conservatives to teach on missions and counseling.
After a while they began to look and talk alike. This was so radically new that an overseas visitor complained that he could not
tell the difference between Pentecostals and conservatives. "They
all look alike," he said. And why shouldn't they? They are children of the same Father, after all!

Failure to give. The world will know that we are followers of
Jesus by our love, and that love begins at home, among ourselves.
Some congregations have a lot; others have next to nothing in
the way of resources. Past a certain point, God will not allow the
wealth of some congregations to exist at the expense of others,
especially when there is some form of contempt being shown on
the part of the larger and stronger congregations. God does not
allow the members of His Body to grow disproportional to each

other. Thus every time a thriving congregation fails to help another congregation that has less, the thriving congregation sets limits on its own growth as well as that of the Body.

One pastor in Argentina understood this principle and donated all his pews to a struggling congregation. He told me that he was also planning to donate the building. When I asked him why he would do that, the pastor replied, "Because I have the gift of faith, and the other pastor doesn't. I can get a building faster than he can."

A pastor in the United Kingdom donated 200 of his specially designed chairs to an ethnic congregation. Those chairs were his pride and joy, but he felt he needed to share them with the poorer group. An Anglo congregation in Ohio donated its fleet of vans to an African-American congregation for the same reason. A group of pastors in northern California underwrote the salary of a pastor whose denomination was planning to let him go because they lacked funds.

God indeed loves a cheerful giver (see 2 Cor. 9:7). The same can be said for congregations. A giving congregation will "have an abundance for every good deed," and will be blessed with more, not less (v. 8).

Build the Bridge Right!

Identify the two persons or groups who are ideologically farthest apart within your city Church. The divide between these two parties represents the gap of disunity in your city. Perhaps their antagonism and belligerence toward one another have thwarted past citywide efforts toward unity. If so, you may have heard statements like, "Until these guys get together and patch up their differences we will not have unity in this city." But this statement is erroneous because it presupposes that for a gap to be bridged, the widest points need to come together first. That is not how you build a bridge to span a gap. The widest points are connected last, not first.

From a scriptural point of view, healing does not begin with those who are involved in divisions but with those who are not: "I hear that there are divisions among you, and in part I believe it. For there must also be factions among you, *that those who are approved may be recognized among you*" (1 Cor. 11:18,19, *NKJV*, emphasis added). Paul viewed divisions as an opportunity for unity to take hold and not the other way around. Those who are approved are the ones who overcome divisions rather than being overcome by them.

The key is to concentrate on bringing together those who are willing to work in unity in order to create a healing middle ground. As a city reacher, you are empowered by God to bridge gaps and to heal wounds. God has already deposited in the hearts of many in your city the truth that there is only one Church. You do not have to fight the battles that consumed others a dozen years ago. You are now free to move on in faith. Do it!

Paradigm #2:
Our City Must Be Reached for Christ Now

> You shall receive power when the Holy Spirit has come upon you; and you shall be My witnesses [beginning] in Jerusalem (Acts 1:8).

Until recently the Church exhibited a serious missiological dysfunction. Congregations would send missionaries to pagan nations, fully convinced that those missionaries could and would reach the natives for Christ. Yet all the while, these same congregations lacked faith that they could reach their own city! This contradiction is beginning to disappear because our understanding of the Great Commission has become sharper on at least two counts.

First, we see in Acts 1:8 that the Great Commission begins with a city, and that city is the city where we live. The Early Church reached cities all over the Roman Empire. You could say that the emphasis of the New Testament is not on church planting but on city reaching. Where a city was reached for Christ, there the Church was planted.

Second, we recognize that the power promised by the Lord in Acts 1:8 is *primarily* power to reach the lost and not power for the sake of improving our own lives. This power is designed to flow in a centrifugal (that which flows toward the periphery) direction, rather than in a centripetal (that which flows toward the center) way. Churches are now starting to realize that they must reach their Jerusalem first in order to have a vortex from which to move outward to the ends of the earth. In the past, Church leaders believed that only cities in foreign lands could be fully reached, whereas now they have begun to believe that their own city must (and most likely will) be reached for Christ first. This paradigm shift makes it easier for city-reaching thrusts to emerge; in fact, they become unavoidable.

A better understanding of key missiological passages such as Acts 1:8 has precipitated this paradigm shift by forcing us to resolve contradictions such as this: If we have received the Holy Spirit, then we have also received the power necessary to reach our city and the world for Christ; so if we have the power, why have we not reached our city for Christ? The answer has to do with the misallocation of the divine power entrusted to us.

Abuse of Power

To illustrate this principle, let me share with you my own pilgrimage in this regard. One of my first prayers shortly after my conversion was for power to overcome sins that had controlled my life. Did I get it? Absolutely! Later on I prayed for power to be a witness to those I studied and worked with, and shortly afterwards, some of those friends came to the Lord. I then prayed for power to find the person that God had prepared to be my wife without having to date anyone else, and the Lord miraculously led me to Ruth. Later on, she and I prayed for power to build a godly Christian home and, again, power was bestowed. Every time I prayed for power I got it. The reason is very simple: When we receive the Holy Spirit, we receive power.

However, the Lord did not promise us a vague, all-purpose kind of power. He specifically promised increasing levels of power for a distinct purpose: witnessing. The level of power available to us depends entirely on *where* we intend to use it. The maximum level is for reaching the ends of the earth. The minimum level of power promised by Jesus is the power to reach our city: "You shall be My witnesses . . . in Jerusalem" (Acts 1:8). For you and me, Jerusalem means the city where we live. The power that set me free from my sins, that allowed me to lead others to Christ, to find the wife He had prepared for me—that power was intended primarily for reaching my city. Sadly, this is the one purpose I did *not* use the power for!

When I finally understood this, I became convicted of self-centeredness and selfishness. I realized that every time I had asked for power, it was to benefit me in some area I had direct control over: my life, my marriage, my family, my ministry, my students, my team. I had never asked for power, much less used it, for its primary purpose of reaching the city. Like the disciples in Acts 1:6, I was more interested in seeing my kingdom established than in taking the kingdom of God to my city and beyond.

I was guilty of abuse of power.

It is a well-proven axiom that if you take care of the city, God will take care of your ministry. If you take care of the county, He will take care of your city. If you take care of the state, He will take care of the county. If you take care of the nations, He will take care of your nation. The farther you cast your net, the safer your position becomes on account of the greater level of power you are entrusted with due to the centrifugal nature of such power.

EVERY PROMISE,
EVERY COMMAND IN
THE BIBLE WILL BE
MISUNDERSTOOD
UNLESS WE INTERPRET
IT IN THE LIGHT OF THE
LORD'S COMMAND
TO WIN THE WORLD
FOR HIM.

The Scriptures in the Light of the Great Commission

I believe the only way to adequately interpret the Scriptures is through the framework of the Great Commission. Every promise, every command in the Bible will be misunderstood (by much or by little) when we fail to interpret it in the light of the Lord's command to win the world for Him. The Bible was written to demonstrate God's love for the lost and His provision for their salvation. Therefore, I contend, the Word can only be fully understood through a missiological grid. God so loved the world that He sent His only begotten Son to save it. In order to understand the Son, the Word Himself, we must view Him through His redemptive mission.

Back in the mid-1990s, Lawrence Khong was a successful pastor in Singapore, his congregation numbering in the thousands.

Along with Ralph Neighbor, Khong was instrumental in popu-
larizing the concept of the cell church, an excellent tool for taking care of the believers in our congregations. Then God began to
speak to him about city reaching. One day, as Khong stood in the
lobby of a busy subway station in Singapore, while thousands of
people were pouring in and out of trains, the Lord asked him,
"Lawrence, can you believe Me for the city—*your* city?" God's presence was so tangible and His words so probing that Lawrence's
heart began to melt. He cried out to God, "Lord, I want to believe
you. Help my unbelief!" Right then and there, God imparted to
Khong the conviction that Singapore could and would be
reached for Christ.

This was no small challenge since Singapore is surrounded by
powerful, militant Muslim nations, and it is illegal to proselytize
Muslims, to evangelize publicly, to advertise services on radio and
TV and to preach using media. Nevertheless, God imparted to
Lawrence the same conviction Jesus stamped on the hearts of the
Early Church. As he left the subway station that day, Khong *knew*
that Singapore was going to be reached for Christ.

Meanwhile, God was working in the hearts and lives of other
pastors in that city-nation, and the pastors there began to pray and
fellowship together, leading to public and private reconciliation. A
prayer summit was held, and I was invited to hold a citywide training seminar on prayer evangelism for the Church in Singapore.
They launched lighthouses of prayer and prayer walking initiatives,
even though these programs were legal impossibilities.

The pastors proposed to the government a walk-a-thon to
raise money for charity. The government granted permission,
and a high-ranking official was invited to wave the starting flag
for thousands of believers, who in reality were doing undercover
prayer walking. Prior to the start, participants were encouraged
to join in warm-up exercises, which were performed to the tune

of Christian songs—in a public field in the middle of the city! The walk-a-thon/prayer walk has since become an annual event.

Tens of thousands of lighthouses of prayer now exist in Singapore. A Love Singapore fund has been established by the different congregations to bless and minister to the city and its inhabitants. Congregations are growing, and the spiritual climate over this city-nation has changed and is now in the hands of the Church.

God has made Singapore the Antioch of Asia, inspiring powerful nation-reaching thrusts in the Philippines, India and Taiwan. I consider Vision 2001, as Singapore's prayer evangelism model is called, to be the premiere prototype for reaching cities and nations. Visit the Vision 2001 web page and view this dynamic and doable model for yourself. Also, Khong has retooled his cell-church concept, with a new focus toward reaching the city. His book *The Apostolic Cell Church* (TMI) is an absolute must-read for those who would reach cities for Christ. The day God met Lawrence Khong at the subway station, He imparted not only faith for Singapore to be reached but also for other nations. It can happen. It is happening!

Cry out to Him right now! When I did, I felt the Spirit of God flooding my innermost parts, convincing me that my city could and should be reached, that the power to do it has been available to me since the day I received Him. I have since heard from hundreds of pastors and leaders who have had a similar experience. They now believe with a passion that their cities can and will be reached.

If *your* city appears to be closed up like Jericho, if reports of giants abound, be aware that this paradigm shift is already in place and God has put hope for the city in the hearts of many.

Be like Caleb, who upon returning from the land of the giants said, "We should by all means go up and take possession of it, for we shall surely overcome it" (Num. 13:30). Pray, "Give me my city, O God." Once you have possessed it, there will be peace in the land, for you will have cleared the land of giants.

Go for it! If you have an ear, hear what the Spirit is saying to the churches: Be My witness in *your* Jerusalem first.

Paradigm #3:
Prayer Evangelism Is the Key to Reaching Our Cities for Christ

I urge that entreaties and prayers, petitions and thanks-givings, be made on behalf of all men (1 Tim. 2:1).

The video *Transformations* by George Otis, Jr. , which depicts four cities that have been literally transformed by the power of God, validates the concept that cities can be reached for Christ. Otis has done a superb job of documenting these spiritual transformations and the infusion of faith in the hearts of millions.

Now people need to know how to facilitate the transition from a spiritual low point, where so many of us find our cities today, to the pinnacle of transformation captured in the video. Without a road map for achieving this, today's inspiration will likely become tomorrow's frustration. This is why before elaborating on this paradigm, we must address two foundational questions: (1) *How* do we reach a city for Christ? and (2) *When* can we say that a city has been reached?

How we reach a city is by building a canopy of prayer over the entire city—block by block, neighborhood by neighborhood—in order to change its spiritual climate. This process reflects strategically what is commanded in 1 Timothy 1:15—2:8. The question of *when* requires a four-part answer—each part representing a higher level of penetration of the gospel:

Level 1: Every lost sheep in the city has a shepherd.
Tangible evidence: A canopy of prayer is in place over the entire city—every block, every neighborhood—and the lost are being prayed for consistently and systematically.
Biblical principle: Bless the lost (see Luke 10:5).

Level 2: Every lost sheep in the city knows who his pastor is.
Tangible evidence: Friendly relationships have been established with the lost through unhurried, unbiased fellowship.
Biblical principle: Fellowship with the lost (see Luke 10:7).

Level 3: The spiritual climate over the city has changed for the better.
Tangible evidence: Godliness has increased as the felt needs of the lost are met through miraculous answers to prayer and acts of kindness, causing the lost to realize that Jesus came into the world to save sinners.
Biblical principle: Meet the felt needs of the lost (see Luke 10:9).

Level 4: The city has been transformed, and the Kingdom is in evidence throughout the city.
Tangible evidence: The Spirit of the Lord is being poured out upon all flesh, and multitudes are coming to the Lord.
Biblical principle: The kingdom of God has come to the city (see Luke 10:9).

Gone are the days when an outsider was expected to come and reach the city for us. There is a growing conviction among members of the Church, especially pastors who pray together, that the grace to reach the city has been deposited *in the city*; and if it takes the whole Church to present the whole gospel to the whole city, *prayer evangelism is the best way to equip the saints to do it*. Since I have discussed prayer evangelism already I will now elaborate on the components for a strategy to implement it at the city-wide level.

In *That None Should Perish*, I suggested six steps to reaching a city for Christ:

1. Establish God's perimeter in the city.
2. Secure God's perimeter.
3. Expand God's perimeter.
4. Infiltrate Satan's perimeter.
5. Attack and destroy Satan's perimeter.
6. Establish God's perimeter where Satan's perimeter used to be.

The first three of these steps must be carried out by the core group of pastors who have embraced the paradigms of one Church in the city and that our city must be reached now. They are the ones who have the vision and the passion. Implementing those three steps will move them from dreaming to actually doing it. However, steps four through six require the mobilization of the whole Church in the city.

A Tried-and-True Method
The most effective method we have seen for mobilizing the Church is a weeklong thrust involving the congregations of those pastors

who pray together. We suggest that on a Sunday morning the Church in the city come together in a large physical place or that individual meeting halls all over town be connected via television. The objective is to inspire, equip, mobilize and deploy the Church to prayer evangelize their city. The heart of the teaching should be from Luke 10:2-9, and Christians should be encouraged to go forth and make peace with the lost and begin to bless them. When I spoke to the Church of Modesto, California, on a Sunday morning to kick off their week-long effort, a local TV station broadcast the signal to 59 congregations, making it a citywide Church meeting.

IT TAKES THE WHOLE CHURCH TO PRESENT THE WHOLE GOSPEL TO THE WHOLE CITY, AND PRAYER EVANGELISM IS THE BEST WAY TO EQUIP THE SAINTS TO DO THIS.

Monday through Wednesday, there should be three one-hour radio broadcasts, ideally scheduled just after the dinner hour for maximum exposure. An ethnically and denominationally diverse group of pastors should host the broadcast, and believers all over the city should be asked to tune in at home. The Monday broadcast should lead Christians to dedicate their homes as lighthouses of prayer. Tuesday's broadcast should focus on the sanctification of homes (see Isa. 6) as the Spirit leads during the broadcast. The focus of Wednesday's broadcast is to mobilize believers to prayer walk their neighborhoods, silently speaking peace over every house and slipping under every door an invitation to a prayer fair that Saturday.

On Thursday and Friday, pastors and intercessors should strengthen the emerging canopy of prayer through prophetic acts such as praying at the gates of the city, speaking peace over the darkest spots in the city, reading the entire Bible out loud in high places, prayer walking every school campus and organizing drive-by prayer caravans. On Saturday, every home in the city should be visited. Connecting the visiting teams by radio will make it very exciting and inspiring as reports of completed tasks are broadcast and teams move over to help where needed. The goal of this exercise is for the Church to visit every home in the city to invite people to the afternoon prayer fair that day (see chapter 6, paradigm #9 for more details on the prayer fair). The following day, Sunday, the Church should gather in a public place around the Lord's Table.

This simple one-week thrust mobilizes the Church and touches an entire city in a very short period of time. Without such an effort, the understanding that there is only one Church in the city and that the city must be reached now will likely not extend far beyond a group of pastors praying together.

If this weeklong prayer evangelism thrust is successfully executed, a canopy of prayer should be in place by the end of the week, securing a level-one penetration of the gospel into the city, as discussed earlier.

Not Bad for a Small Group

Reaching this first level represents a major milestone for the Church in a city. Visualize for a moment the tremendous potential in this exercise: If 10 pastors, whose congregations together comprise 5,000 members, mobilize their people to pray for 100 people each, their combined sphere of spiritual influence becomes 500,000 people! Not bad for a group of 10 pastors!

Let me encourage you to move forward and do it. No matter how small the initial canopy turns out to be, it will be bigger than anything you have now. If your city has a population of 500,000 and your congregation numbers only 200, do not let the disparity in these figures discourage you. Motivate, equip, mobilize and train your flock to become shepherds over the people within their sphere of influence, and challenge other pastors to do the same. If they are able to mobilize another 800 members, that's 1,000 participants. You can now realistically anticipate a canopy of prayer over 100,000 unbelievers, or *20 percent of the population!*

Though some may suggest that you have failed to reach the city because *only* 100,000 people have been reached, the effort is worth it. It is always better to aim at a star and miss than to aim at a skunk and hit! It is far preferable to face the Lord having reached only 100,000 than to bury your talent and be rebuked by Him (see Matt. 25:25-30).

Prayer evangelism is the way to accomplish this. Because it can be done, it must be done! Go for it.

Paradigm #4:
Identificational Repentance

"Identificational repentance" is a term coined by John Dawson and superbly explained in his book *Healing America's Wounds* (Regal Books). Identificational repentance consists of the spiritual ownership of corporate sins committed by people in the group we belong to, in order to effectively repent on their behalf to the injured parties as a prelude to making restoration. This kind of repentance enables the Church in the city to deal effectively, in a way that is meaningful and relevant to the injured parties, with iniquities such as racism and bigotry, the roots of which precede our generation.

In 1 Timothy 2:1-8, we are commanded to pray everywhere for all men, "lifting up holy [clean] hands . . . without wrath and dissension" (v. 8). In practical terms, this means that to prayer evangelize, we first must rid ourselves of anger and reverse its consequences (dissension) by mending broken relationships.

Although this sounds very straightforward and simple, complications arise when the iniquity at hand involves not just individuals but socially conflicted groups—e.g., men/women, white/ethnic, management/labor. Complications are further compounded when the onset of the initial offense preceded our generation, forcing us to face anger whose roots seem to be beyond our reach.

Thus the question, "Do we have to deal with a sin we did not commit ourselves but the consequences of which are still in evidence and, if so, how?" This question becomes even more complex when we add Western individualism to the mix with its focus on the personal dimension of sin at the expense of the corporate one, creating a spiritual puzzle of gigantic proportions.

Taking an X Ray of Ephesians

Identificational repentance and its ability to deal with corporate sins is an essential tool that we must use if we are to reach our cities. We can see this in the book of Ephesians. This letter, written to a Church that had reached a city (see Acts 19), identifies six corporate gaps that must be bridged before we can effectively confront the rulers, powers and spiritual forces of wickedness in the heavenly places (see Eph. 6:12). The six gaps in question look like this:

Gap	Groups Representing the Gap
Ethnic (Eph. 2)	Jews vs. Gentiles
Denominational (Eph. 3)	The Lost vs. the Saints
Ministerial (Eph. 4:1-16)	Apostles vs. Prophets, Evangelists, Pastors and Teachers
Gender (Eph. 5:22-33)	Husbands vs. Wives
Age (Eph. 6:1-4)	Parents vs. Children
Marketplace (Eph. 6:5-9)	Masters vs. Slaves

Paul instructs us to wrestle against the spiritual forces of wickedness *after* he has shown us how to bridge these six corporate gaps. In Ephesians 6:10 (*NKJV*), after showing how to bridge the gap between masters and slaves, he admonishes, "Finally, my brethren, be strong in the Lord and in the power of His might," to be able to stand firm in the evil day. Paul is talking about spiritual warfare of the most intense nature—against the devil himself.

His exhortation here has two components: to be strong in the Lord and to be strong in the power of His might. Even though these things are complementary, they are definitely two different things.

It Takes a Strong Person to Build Bridges

To be "strong in the Lord" refers specifically to the bridging of the six gaps mentioned above, because in God there are no such divisions. In Him there is neither Jew nor Gentile, neither Paul nor Cephas nor Apollos, neither male nor female, neither master nor slave, meaning that no group has higher claim than the other. When we become strong in the Lord, we are able to see each other as God sees us, without the divisions caused by sin. The anger that kept us separated has now been eliminated by the power of the Cross. This is the *defensive* dimension of spiritual warfare that secures our inner perimeter by voiding the jurisdictions given to the devil through the anger that created those gaps (see Eph. 4:26,27). But this is only half of the equation.

The other half is to be strong "in the power of His might." This is the *offensive* dimension necessary to engage and defeat the forces of evil in the heavenly places. However, no such offensive should be undertaken until all the gaps listed in chapters 2 through 6 have been bridged. Since these gaps and the division they represent reflect conflicts between groups, not just individuals, this is where identificational repentance comes in.

Can We Repent for Another Person's Sins?

One of the objections to the biblical validity of identificational repentance is rooted in the belief that a person can confess someone else's sin but cannot repent for it because only the actual perpetrator can do that. When it comes to personal sins, this is correct; but that is not the case regarding corporate sins. God deals with groups as much as He deals with individuals. This is an area where Western individualism prevents us from seeing the reality of the corporate dimension of life in general and in the Scriptures in particular.

Western theology tends to be one-dimensional, focused on the individual and his relationship with God. This approach overlooks the fact that there are plenty of examples in the Bible where God dealt with groups of people—blessing them or punishing them—on account of the actions of an individual. Abraham believed God and, as a consequence, nations were blessed. Achan sinned during the looting of Jericho, and he and his entire family suffered mortal consequences. Moses, on more than one occasion, interceded before God for the sins of Israel, and God spared the nation. Likewise, Nehemiah repented for the sins of his forefathers. Sin has a corporate dimension—and corporate consequences. If grace is God's remedy for sin, then in order to be effective, grace must also have corporate benefits.

Absolved Individually, Condemned Corporately

Even though contemporary white people in America do not own slaves, the sin of slavery is a white man's sin and its consequences are still in evidence all over. Our black brethren are far worse off today because their ancestors were exploited by ours yesterday. We tend to see slavery as a sin of the past, but the millions of people whose ancestors have been abused by ours live daily with the consequences of this sin. White folks absolve themselves individually, but they stand condemned corporately, even though they may have difficulty seeing it that way.

This difficulty is compounded by the fact that white folks are one of the few people groups who do not have a people-group mentality. For instance, when asked their name, a white person gives his or her name, and that is the end of the story. However, when a nonwhite person answers the same question, an echo in his or her mind adds, "And I am an African-American (or Hispanic or Asian or Native American)." This is so because these people see themselves as part of a bigger social unit—their people group—and this has a direct impact on how they process reality, especially in the area of injustice.

What You See Depends on Your Color

This is why whites and nonwhites experienced such divergent reactions when they watched the video of the 1991 beating of Rodney King, the African-American man savagely beaten by white police officers during a traffic stop in Los Angeles.

Many whites saw only a black ex-con who was in violation of parole, getting a bit roughed up by police officers who just happened to be white. To whites, the incident represented an issue between individuals: Rodney King and the officers who beat him.

African-Americans reacted quite differently. What they registered was the beating of the black race by the white race. At that moment, they saw the historical corporate iniquities of the latter revisited on the former—hence their explosive reaction when the white officers were exonerated in court.

This inability of most white people to connect with their own people group prevents them from seeing the need to *repent* for the sins of their group rather than just confess them. One way to correct this is for white Christians to seek out an ethnic person to become their soul brother/sister and to develop a life-long friendship in order to learn to see and experience the corporate dimension of life.

The Difference Between Race and Ethnicity

A second area of difficulty regarding the ethnic gap is our failure to distinguish between race and ethnicity. Race is transferred by genes; ethnicity is transferred via culture. Failure to distinguish between race and ethnicity has led us to assume incorrectly that by adding "color" instead of substance, we have bridged the ethnic gap in our congregations and staffs.

I have heard pastors say, "I have a fully integrated staff. My associates are Filipino, African-American, Asian and Hispanic." The problem is that they all behave like whites! Fully integrated cannot mean simply giving permission to people of different races to come into our circle to adopt our lifestyle. This is no better than what happens at the neighborhood level when non-white people are allowed (or tolerated) to move in as long as they are willing to blend into the prevailing white culture.

Right Intention, Wrong Results

This is what happened in President Lyndon Johnson's social program, the Great Society. By making it possible for *the most promising nonwhite leaders* to move out of their ancestral neighborhoods into traditionally white areas, nonwhite groups were deprived of their most talented people, the ones capable of mentoring young people—a concept central to most nonwhite cultures. It is no wonder that ethnic neighborhoods quickly turned into ghettos.

Such ethnocentrism is no better than the attitude of the Judaizers with whom Paul had so much trouble. They believed that Gentiles could be saved, as long as they became *culturally* Jewish. This is what is going on today in many "integrated" circles. Ethnics are welcomed as long as they adopt the white man's lifestyle and culture.

To correct this ethnocentrism—this undervaluing of ethnic cultures—we need to keep in mind that nonwhites perceive whites' actions through a three-level grid: participation, partnership and leadership. The first level is the one we are most familiar with. Predominantly white congregations often make a point of participating in events and programs together with nonwhite congregations. The area where improvement is needed is to ensure this participation is a two-way street. Instead of always expecting nonwhites to come to our place, we must also go to theirs—joyfully and without fear!

The other two levels are far less developed. Partnership will require give-and-take and treating nonwhites with the deference and respect that working partners are treated with in corporations. They need to be consulted before decisions are made. We cannot set the table, choose the menu, assign the seating and pay for the meal and expect them to enjoy it.

However, the highest level is leadership. This is when nonwhites lead and whites *follow*. This level cannot be attained in the first pass; but if we keep in mind this three-level grid, we will not be content with inviting their participation, and we will begin to make progress towards partnership and leadership by nonwhites.

The need to bridge the ethnic gap and the other five before engaging the forces of evil is consistent with the exhortation in 1 Timothy 2:8 to rid ourselves of the dissentions resulting from wrath. Identificational repentance is God's provision for this. What is the alternative? Please allow me to show how ugly things could get by painting a picture in which the six gaps are not bridged: We will find ourselves in an ethnically divided and segregated Church made up of warring factions divided over minor points of doctrine and practice, under the destructive leadership of competing ministers in a context of unresolved abuse affecting men and women, parents and children, rich and poor. Who would believe our message then? It is no wonder that Jesus prayed that we may all be one so that "the world may believe" (John. 17:21).

Praise God, this picture is beginning to improve as groups of people repent before each other, whether in the solitude of a small church building or at a gigantic Promise Keepers rally. Identificational repentance is God's tool for doing this. Let us use it!

Notes
1. John Isaacs pastors South Bay Covenant Church in Campbell, California. Michael Griffiths is a member of Harvest Evangelism who has pioneered prayer walking initiatives and the March for Jesus in Northern California.
2. Three months later 312 people—pastors, leaders, and intercessors—chartered a ship and "prayer sailed" around the bay for five hours. They celebrated communion on board, performed identificational repentance and proclaimed the lordship of Jesus over the region. For a detailed account, read Bill and Pam Malone's *Come to the Waters* (PrayUSA).

RECENT PARADIGMS

The Church is found in buildings, mainly on Sundays;
but it does not belong there. The Church belongs outdoors—
that is, all over the city.

The five paradigms discussed in this chapter are as valid and biblical as the recent paradigms we have already talked about; but
these represent shifts in thinking of a more modern vintage.
These *recent paradigms*, which are only now beginning to take
hold throughout the Church, bring home a most refreshing
point: *The Church does not belong in a building but is to be found all
over the city.*

   Kites do not fly in attics, but in the sky. They may be stored
in attics, but that does not make the attic their natural habitat.
Boats do not sail on a trailer that is pulled along the road; they
sail on the water. Boats may sometimes be seen being hauled on
a trailer, but that is not their defining locale. Likewise, the

Church is found in buildings, mainly on Sundays, but it does not belong there. The Church belongs outdoors—that is, all over the city. Let me tell you a story that will illustrate this more clearly.

The church picnic had been planned expertly. Workers had been assigned to every age group, and the finest specialists were put in charge of logistics, games, ministry and sports. The right equipment was secured and transported to the picnic site. The entire congregation showed up on time and with great expectation. Everything was in place, and everyone was looking forward to a great time. But 30 minutes into the picnic it began to rain torrentially, and everybody and everything had to be moved in a hurry to a nearby barn.

Making the best of a bad situation, the leaders divided the barn into sectors. They put the barbecue pits and the serving tables toward the back of the barn. In the center of the barn they set up the table games. To the right they created a children's area. Next to the children, they positioned the youth and their overpowering worship band. The adult section was placed closer to the exit, with a subsection reserved for the intercessors; and between them and the main door, a sports area was hastily set up with improvised volleyball and mini soccer fields.

Unfortunately, no one was happy. Most of the games and all of the sports had been designed to be played outdoors rather than indoors. The smoke from the barbecue pits stung the people's eyes. What to the youth was exciting music was a disgusting clang to most adults in such close quarters. Things reached the boiling point when a deflected soccer ball hit the dessert table, unleashing a cascade of meringue and whipped cream with plenty of mousse as flotsam. Tempers flared, unkind words were exchanged and what could have been a memorable day became an infamous one. Why? *Because what went on inside the barn was meant to take place outdoors.*

This is true of the Church today. Many of the problems that plague her would not be problems at all *if* the Church were to operate more outdoors than indoors. The latter exemplifies the erroneous notion that the city should come to the church. It is the other way around: *The Church must go to the city.*

Do Not Wait for the World to Come to You

This tendency toward self-centeredness was present in the Church from the very beginning. When Jesus told the disciples to wait in Jerusalem until the Holy Spirit had come upon them, they immediately asked the wrong question: "Lord, is it at this time You are restoring the kingdom to Israel?" (Acts 1:6). The disciples' interest in the restoration of the Kingdom had to do with the ancient days, especially Solomon's time, when Jerusalem was the center of the world. If such a restoration were to take place, they reasoned, the entire world would come to Jerusalem, where the disciples would have a platform to tell the world about Christ. It seems the disciples were hoping for something to catch the attention of the world to make the world come *to them.*

Jesus had something different in mind: His disciples would instead go *to the world.* They were to reach Jerusalem first and from there to move outwardly to Judea and Samaria and to keep on moving until they had reached the ends of the earth. Jesus never intended for the Church to be a monument to be gazed at but, rather, a *movement* that would sweep up everything in its path. He was definitely not thinking of a barn picnic!

In spite of Jesus' clear admonition, it still took 14 years for the disciples to leave Jerusalem for good, and then not voluntarily but as the result of persecution. It seems they liked living in a city that had seen its share of the power of God over the centuries. Nevertheless, the most dramatic power encounters recorded in the book of Acts happened *after* they left Jerusalem; hence the wisdom of *going to* the lost rather than *waiting for* them (see Acts 8—12).

Until recently the Church has been stuck in the rut of Acts 1:6, working hard to produce the neatest, best-organized, most appealing barn picnics. We have consistently applied divine power to make our presentations bigger and better, hoping that the lost will take notice and come into our tidy little barns. Praise God, this is another paradigm that is beginning to change. The paradigm shifts I describe in this chapter show that the Church is finally making its way out of the barn.

Paradigm #5:
The Church Was Not Born in the Upper Room but in the Marketplace

When this sound occurred, the multitude came together. But Peter, taking his stand with the eleven, raised his voice and declared to them. So then, those who had received his word were baptized; and there were added that day about three thousand souls (Acts 2:6,14,41).

The Upper Room belongs in the Christian Hall of Fame along with the manger from the stable in Bethlehem. Jesus was born in the manger; that is a fact. The Upper Room is considered the place where the Church was born. I have nothing but reverence for the Upper Room, but I do not believe it is the Church's birthplace. Great harm has come out of this misconception. When the Holy Spirit fell on the disciples in the Upper Room, the first thing He did was to *get them out* rather than *keep them in*. This is a crucial point.

Babies are conceived in their mother's womb, but they are not born until they have come out of the womb. Likewise, the Church was conceived (and fully developed the way a baby is) in the Upper Room, but it was not born until the disciples went out into the marketplace where the Word of God was preached and 3,000 men believed in Christ.[1] This point is key, because as long as we believe that the Church was born inside four walls, we will always need four walls to have a church. Worse yet, this will cause us to confuse the church building with the *eklesia*—the gathering of believers. They are two completely different things.

This paradigm shift is crucial for city reaching.

A congregation of 1,000 members are, during most of the week, already strategically placed in neighborhoods, workplaces and campuses all over the city. Because of this strategic deployment, they are in position to become pastors to scores of people within their spheres of influence. If each member takes responsibility for 100 unsaved acquaintances and friends, the combined sphere of influence of that congregation will encompass 100,000 people!

However, when the Church and the church building are closely associated in our minds to the point of being perceived almost as interchangeable, an evangelistic disaster occurs. Believers are expected to invite sinners to a church building to hear a preacher, in hopes that these lost souls will receive the Lord. Unfortunately, very few do, and those that do require significant attention and maintenance to keep them coming to the building!

Jesus presented the kingdom of God not as something that people need to be brought into but as something that comes near to them: "Say to them, 'The kingdom of God *has come near to you*'" (Luke 10:9, emphasis added). Consequently, the Church needs to go to the people.

Soon after the Church was born, the first Christians filled the city of Jerusalem with the teaching of the gospel message (see Acts 5:28). How did they do it? In the Temple and house to house—in public as much as in private places—they held church daily, not weekly!

> And day by day continuing with one mind in the temple, and breaking bread from house to house, they were taking their meals together with gladness and sincerity of heart, praising God, *and having favor with all the people* (Acts 2:46,47, emphasis added).

Please notice the dynamic nature of the Church, how by doing church house-to-house they gained favor with all the people. This was dynamic, God-driven evangelism: "And the Lord was adding to their number day by day those who were being saved" (v. 47).

Church is too good to be kept under wraps. It belongs all over town.

An Ecclesiastical Lockout

Richard Gazowsky, the pastor of Voice of Pentecost, in San Francisco, California, realized some time ago that his parishioners were somehow confused on this issue. Worse yet, he believed, the pride they felt in coming to church—that is, to the church building—in such a godless city made them too "religious." Gazowsky decided to do something drastic about the situation. In fact, what he did is so extreme that I am not sure you should try to replicate it. I am simply reporting it because it eloquently illustrates the point under discussion.

Richard put his parishioners on a 40-day "church-building fast"—he instructed them not to come to the church building for 40 days. If they did, they would find the doors locked.

During this unusual fast—the ecclesiastical equivalent of a labor lockout—members were asked not to spend time with other Christians or listen to Christian radio or TV or read Christian magazines; instead they were instructed to invest time in befriending neighbors and going to sporting and social events with them. In addition, every week when the members stopped by the church office to bring their tithes and offerings, Richard gave them a map showing a section of the city where they were to place doorknob hangers displaying this message: "God loves you and so do we. If you need prayer, please contact our church at this phone number. If you come by, we will gladly give you a Bible."

The goal was to make contact with every home in San Francisco—a major undertaking for a relatively small congregation. Nevertheless, minutes away from midnight on the 40th day, in the midst of a fierce storm, the last home in the city was contacted, bringing the total to about 261,900. The results were extraordinary: 8,600 people called for prayer, 10,000 Bibles were given away, 4,100 inquired about salvation and 150 were baptized immediately.[2] And this happened in San Francisco, of all places! Richard proved that when we move the picnic outdoors, everybody wants to join in!

Blessings During Rush Hour

Eduardo Lorenzo, a Baptist pastor in the city of Adrogue, Argentina, did something similar. On December 23, 1998, he deployed 550 believers representing 12 congregations in one of the major train stations in Buenos Aires, the equivalent of Victoria Station in London. At exactly 6 P.M., the beginning of rush hour, they all began to sing "Hallelujah," first softly and then in a crescendo, until the entire lobby was filled with their voices *and the tangible presence of God!*

Since this was rush hour, thousands of commuters heard and saw the singing. Many of them stood watching, a few weeping. Christians blessed the commuters as they boarded the trains, and small bands of believers boarded the same trains. They scattered to the various cars and made it known that they were there to minister to the passengers. In the end, almost 7,000 people were witnessed to personally; 6,736 accepted prayer for felt needs; and 1,704 received the Lord *publicly*. Everybody seemed to enjoy this outdoor picnic.

Paradigm #6:
Prayer Is Also a Public Activity

Therefore, I want the men in every place to pray, lifting up holy hands, without wrath and dissension (1 Tim 2:8).

In the same fashion that the legitimate need for a building in which to meet obscures the fact that the Church belongs all over the city, an overemphasis on the private dimension of prayer undermines and quite often destroys the public dimension—the dimension essential for prayer evangelism. If it is harmful to confine the Church (eklesia) to four walls, it is even more harmful to confine prayer to the prayer closet. Doing so deprives the already restrained Church of a powerful biblical tool to touch the lost: public prayer.

A word study on prayer in the Bible reveals more examples of public prayer than of private prayer. This does not mean that people did not pray in private, but it does prove that public prayer has a stronger biblical basis than we have been led to believe.

The Lost Need to Hear Us Pray

We find several instances in the Bible in which the salvation of the lost was at stake when public prayer came to the rescue. Elijah, in his memorable power encounter with the prophets of Baal, did not say, "Okay folks, now close your eyes and bow your heads while I get into this port-a-closet to pray." On the contrary, he prayed loud and clear in full view and within earshot of everybody.

Jesus also saw public prayer as very strategic. Prior to raising Lazarus from the dead, He approached the Father and said something like, "Father, in a few moments I am going to raise My voice in prayer. Please, do not think that I doubt that You always hear Me. I know You do. But I need to pray out loud for the people to hear My prayer, so that when You answer, they will know that You heard Me" (see John 11:42).

Paul also gave specific instructions to take our prayers all over the city: "I desire therefore that the men pray everywhere" (1 Tim. 2:8, *NKJV*). Everywhere means in every place in the city, not all over the church building. When Paul and his companions arrived in Philippi and went looking for a prayer meeting, where did they go? Down by the riverside—hardly a private place (see Acts 16:13). Later, Paul and Silas were thrown in jail, where they prayed out loud. How did the nonbelievers who were present respond? "And the prisoners were listening to them" (Acts 16:25).

This recent paradigm shift is changing the way we pray. As Christians begin to pray publicly, they are finding that their prayers are welcomed, not resented, by the lost.

Have You Prayed for Your Waitress?

A group of Christian leaders who were having lunch in a Dallas restaurant asked their waitress if she had any needs they could pray for. She told them she needed a car. They asked her to specify what kind of car she wanted. When she said a black Nissan, they held hands and prayed for it in her presence. Halfway through the prayer, they were interrupted by loud sobbing. The waitress was crying. Through her tears she said, "Nobody has ever prayed for me. I am deeply moved." She received the Lord that day along with four other employees who had witnessed the public prayer.

On another occasion, my friend Rick Heeren and I tried to get something to eat in a hotel where I was staying, only to be turned away because the restaurant was about to close for the day.[3] We were directed to the bar instead. As we entered the bar, we noticed that the bartender, a woman, looked sad and overwhelmed. When she came to take our order, we asked if she needed prayer for anything. She looked at us, perplexed, as if trying to decide whether we were for real or not. She asked, "You're not serious, are you?" When we told her that we meant it, she literally fell on her knees by our table and said, "I desperately need prayer. Please do it!" She told us she needed a different job. We prayed for it. Within 24 hours, God opened the door for a new job, and she came to understand that "Jesus came into the world to save *sinners*" (1 Tim. 1:15, emphasis added).

A Dream Team or a Nightmare?

Understanding the public dimension of prayer and the fact that the marketplace is the Church's natural habitat is crucial to prayer evangelism. Let me illustrate this with an example from the world of sports.

Larry Bird, Michael Jordan, Magic Johnson, Charles Barkley and other top NBA players were brought together during the 1984 Olympic Games to form the best basketball team ever.

They were called the Dream Team. This was the most fantastic conglomeration of athletic talent ever assembled—absolutely unbeatable. I know this because I watched our Argentina national team play against them and lose by more points than I care to remember.

But what if a restriction had been imposed on the Dream Team, prohibiting its members from going past center court toward their own basket? They still would have played a stunning defensive game. Even shooting from half-court, they would have sunk enough baskets to win most, if not all, of their games. That is how good those guys were! However, if these were just average players, the team would have lost all its games under such conditions. The reason is very simple: It takes star players to regularly sink baskets from half-court.

EVANGELISM IN THE CHURCH HAS LARGELY BEEN LEFT TO THE STAR PLAYERS, WHILE THE REST WATCH FROM THE SIDELINES.

Evangelism in the Church has largely been left to the star players, those extraordinary people capable of scoring from 50 meters away, while the rest watch from the sidelines. When they have shot the ball, the Church has scored big. When ordinary folks have tried to do it, the Church too often has come up short. But the Church is now rediscovering the public dimension of prayer, enabling all its players to dribble all over the court to score at will. The Church no longer plays the best defensive game in town; we have gone on the offensive with all our players shooting and scoring, and the scoreboard bears testimony to our success. The tide is turning. The Church is winning!

Paradigm #7:
The Fold Is Not Equal to the Flock

And seeing the multitudes, He felt compassion for them, because they were distressed and downcast like sheep without a shepherd (Matt. 9:36).

Pastors for the most part have done a superb job ministering to the people under their care while working for very little pay, under taxing circumstances, often unappreciated and always at great personal cost. There is no question as to the wonderful quality of pastoring throughout the Church and the outstanding level of commitment of pastors in general. Unfortunately, a major mistake has been made in understanding the size of the flocks entrusted to these same pastors. For centuries, the Church's conception of the flock has been too restrictive and thus the majority of the lambs have been neglected. To understand this let us take a look at a very revealing passage.

In John 21:15 (NKJV), when Jesus asked Peter, "Do you love Me?" and Peter replied in the affirmative, Jesus said to him, "Feed my lambs." Traditionally, many have interpreted this to mean that Jesus appointed Peter to be the earthly head of the Church that Jesus Himself was about to leave behind. However, this interpretation is far too narrow and is misleading.

Jesus was very specific in His instructions: "Feed my lambs." What does it mean to feed or to tend His lambs? The lambs that need feeding the most are not the ones that are in the fold but the ones outside of it—that is, the lost lambs. In the parable of the good shepherd, the 99 lambs are left in the pasture, with its abundance of food, while the good shepherd goes looking for the lamb that is lost and most likely now hungrier than the others (see Matt. 18:12-14).

Passion for People

Too often the Church has concentrated on caring for the saints at the expense of the lost. I remember seeing an ad for a well-known seminary in which the photo of a famous national speaker who graduated from that seminary was accompanied by this caption: "Our passion is the people in the pews." As nice as this sounds, it misses the mark on at least two counts: First, those in the pews represent a minority of the lambs entrusted to us; and second, if we have done our job half-right, those in the pews should be able to feed themselves. The lost lambs need our care more, and they need it urgently. That is where our passion should be.

The flock that Jesus entrusted to us is made up of two kinds of sheep: the found and the lost. The former are inside the fold, while the latter are outside, lost but still part of the flock. We have erred in considering the fold to be the entire flock. This is a mistake. The flock and the fold are not one and the same. The flock is made up of the population of the city, the majority of whom are lost and spiritually hungry. The fold, much smaller, is occupied by those who are saved. When Jesus instructed Peter to feed His lambs, He was speaking primarily of those outside the fold, because they are the ones in greater need of feeding.

A Mall Pastor

A pastor in the south of England decided to introduce himself to shop owners at the city mall as their pastor. He asked their forgiveness for having neglected them in the past and announced that he would be making pastoral rounds regularly. At first the shop owners did not know how to respond to this; but assuming that no trouble could come from it, they quietly acquiesced. Every day the pastor went by the mall, stopping at every shop, looking for opportunities to minister and soliciting prayer requests. Soon he was praying daily for shop owners and occasionally for a customer referred by them. Today, this pastor is highly esteemed as the Mall Chaplain, and some there proudly introduce him as "my chaplain."

This pastor even developed an informal friendship with both a homosexual and a lesbian. As he showed them unconditional love and acceptance, they began to trust him. This led first to some light interaction on spiritual matters, which eventually led to more elaborate requests for prayer. Gradually, these two fell in love *with each other*, and they asked the pastor to perform the marriage ceremony. The pastor agreed and suggested premarital counseling. In one of the first sessions, he introduced the importance of faith in God as a pillar for a lasting marriage. Then he suggested they take the Alpha Course.[4] Halfway through the course, both of them received the Lord and renounced their old lifestyles. What a change! One never knows what extraordinary things may happen when we venture outside of the fold.

Paradigm #8:
Pastors Are Called to Pastor the City, Not Just the Church

Behold, you have filled Jerusalem with your teaching (Acts 5:28).

God is always inclusive and expansive when it comes to caring for the lost. The heart of the city in New Testament times was the marketplace, and that is where Paul and his associates concentrated their efforts in order to touch the city and the surrounding region. The city was their primary objective. This is a very important point because it reveals a serious contemporary problem: We are planting churches to pastor saints rather than to pastor the city. Or, worse yet, we plant a "church" to fulfill our pastoral call, with no compelling regard for the lost.

Often, church planters scout a city and ascertain that though a number of good churches are there already, a new one would likely do well, so they go ahead and plant one for the sake of future members but seldom for the sake of the city. As if to emphasize the purity of their motivations, they state that they are not interested in quantity but only in quality, their main objective being to establish a testimony. This was not Paul's strategy. He could have planted thousands of new congregations between Jerusalem and Illyricum, but he chose not to. Why? Because his primary objective was to reach cities, not to plant churches where "Christ was already named" (Rom. 15:20) as we do today.

This is not to say that planting churches was not important to Paul. It was. However, he saw the Church the way a farmer sees the barn: as a servant to the harvest and never as a substitute for it. Beginning with Acts 1:8, the thrust was always for reaching cities and regions, and churches were planted as a result.

How Big Is Your Congregation?

More and more pastors are beginning to see the city with its many clusters of lost people—schools, bars, hospitals, city hall, jails, schools, parks—as their parish. They understand that everyone in town is a member of the flock entrusted to them, even though most of the flock is not in the fold. Furthermore, these pastors are seeing with increased clarity that, like the shepherd in the parable of the lost sheep, they need to prioritize the lost over the found (without neglecting the latter).

Cacho Castels, a pastor in San Nicolas, Argentina, was asked how large his congregation was. He replied, "We pastor 130,000 people. Some of them are prostitutes, others homosexuals. Most of them lie and cheat, but they are all under our care." He was referring, of course, to the population of the whole city that he and his fellow pastors have come to see as their flock. When they realized this for the first time during the weeklong thrust described in chapter 1, the pastors of San Nicolas fell on their faces before God and renounced the spiritual myopia and self-centeredness that had caused them to neglect the most needy members of the flock entrusted to them by Jesus. They then went to seven leading city officials to ask forgiveness for having neglected them. They visited the mayor, the chief of police, the Catholic bishop, the editor of the town newspaper, the director of public health and both owners of the local radio and TV stations.

The reaction of these leaders to the pastors' claim of spiritual jurisdiction over them? The mayor asked them to pray for him regularly. The chief of police requested permission to send police officers to be prayed for. The newspaper editor printed, at cost, the literature needed to visit every house in town with an invitation to the prayer fair. The owners of the radio and TV stations invited the pastors as guests on live programs to pray for the people in the city. The director of public health appointed two pastors to the board of health to pray for the doctors and for the sick when the doctors were unable to help them. The most dramatic response of all came from the Catholic bishop, who humbly asked the pastors to pray for him to preach the Word of God every time he spoke to the pilgrims (close to one million a year) who visit the shrine.

Best of all, thousands of people attended the prayer fair held on Saturday of that history-making week. Most of them were prayed for personally, and several hundred received the Lord. Difficult to believe? Perhaps, but absolutely real. Jesus knew best when He told us to take care of His hungry lambs.

Who Else Is on Board?

Understanding that our primary focus should be the city with its multitudes of lost people has two powerful, healthy effects. The first is a stronger impetus toward unity. When pastors realize they are called to shepherd the entire city instead of just one congregation, the question they ask right away is, "Who else is on board?" Triggered by the realization that they cannot pastor the Lord's flock by themselves, the need for unity in the Church becomes compelling and unavoidable!

The second effect is a healthier understanding of pastoral jurisdiction. When it comes to pastoring the Church, we know that God has given leaders the authority and the resources necessary to carry out the assignments entrusted to them. Unfortunately, if pastors fail to understand that their jurisdiction extends beyond the congregation to the city, they end up seeing the city as beyond their reach, and a feeling of spiritual impotence sets in, making them easy prey for discouragement and even depression.

WHEN PASTORS REALIZE THEY ARE CALLED TO SHEPHERD THE ENTIRE CITY, THE NEED FOR UNITY IN THE CHURCH BECOMES COMPELLING AND UNAVOIDABLE!

This happened to Elijah immediately after his tremendous victory over the prophets of Baal (see 1 Kings 18:24-38). He fled in panic from a woman, Jezebel, and he remained discouraged, even though he was being fed by angels (see 1 Kings 19:4-8)! Elijah was so depressed that he hid in a cave and failed to comprehend the lesson God was teaching him through a dramatic display of the forces of nature. Why? Because he wrongly concluded that he was the only prophet left.

God had two lessons for Elijah: First, he was not alone; there were 7,000 other men he had failed to notice. Second, God's lordship extends to everybody, even to those outside the circle of believers. To drive this point home, God commanded Elijah to anoint three leaders—Hazael, as king of Aram; Jehu, as king of Israel; and Elisha, as his replacement as national prophet. God assured Elijah that these three men would finish the job that had so overwhelmed him. I find it fascinating that two of the three to be anointed were evil people!

The moment Elijah realized he had the jurisdiction, he understood that he also had the tools—authority and anointing—to handle the situation at hand. When pastors understand that the city falls under their jurisdiction, they are able to view the city positively and confidently.

Mercy Is Easier to Understand Than Grace

As pastors understand more and more that their primary call is to the flock and that their activities in the fold must flow from that call, they will begin to generate tangible acts of mercy to prove to the most vulnerable lambs, the lost ones, that we really care for them. Mercy is the key to reaching the lost because its tangible nature is something unbelievers can understand better, faster and easier than they can comprehend grace.

The National Association of Women (NOW) is one of the most liberal and anti-Christian organizations in the nation's capital, with a solid record of strong opposition to anything and everything that committed Christians stand for. I remember that during the Promise Keepers' Stand in the Gap meeting in Washington, DC, in 1998, NOW president Patricia Ireland was quite active, giving scalding interviews to the media to express her opposition and disgust at the men—over a million of us— praying at the Mall.

However, when Mother Teresa spoke to NOW members in Washington, she received a standing ovation and excellent reviews in the media. She preached the same message that Christian representatives preach every day. So why did Mother Teresa receive a standing ovation from NOW? I suggest that it is because Mother Teresa's message was clothed in mercy—she spoke against a backdrop of merciful acts for people outside her fold. On the other hand, much of what most national Christian leaders say, though it makes theological sense, does not register with the lost sheep. The lost see them coming, swinging a staff, and immediately sense that they are out to punish them.

If we were to speak to the lost sheep with the same love, acceptance and comfort we give to those in the fold, the lost would readily and hungrily accept our embrace.

Paradigm #9:
It Is Possible to Change the Spiritual Climate over a City

First of all, then, I urge that entreaties and prayers, petitions and thanksgivings, be made on behalf of all men,

for kings and all who are in authority, in order that we
may lead a tranquil and quiet life in all godliness and
dignity. This is good and acceptable in the sight of God
our Savior (1 Tim. 2:1-3).

I have discussed the biblical basis for this paradigm in chapter 3,
and I have described a strategy for achieving this. Therefore, I
will not repeat myself except to say that changing the spiritual
climate over our cities must be the compelling and driving objective for every city-reaching initiative. This objective must be kept
in mind at all times, or we will fall short of God's design for our
mission.

Under paradigm 3, I introduced a four-level definition of a
city that has been reached for Christ. Changing the climate is
level 3. Once this level is reached, the resulting change in climate
sets the stage for the transformation that is the main characteristic of level 4: The kingdom of God is in evidence all over the
city. Changing the climate over the city is the prerequisite for
city transformation. There is no substitute for it.

Let us now focus on the crucial role of communication in a
strategy to change the spiritual climate. To put this in perspective, we must review what God has done in the past decade along
a continuum I call *unity-mission-communication*.

Unity Must Have Mission

God is now actively bringing pastors together in cities all over
the world. This trend is irreversible; disunity is on the way out.
Once the devil knew he could no longer keep us apart, he adopted an alternative strategy: to encourage *unity* without *mission*.
Unity without mission means pastors have no other agenda
than coming together. Far too often in recent years, not having

an agenda has been embraced as the ultimate expression of spir-
ituality. The no-agenda emphasis soon became an agenda in
itself, and in some places, it sidetracked what God was doing
with the pastors.

Blessedly, this is being corrected. More and more, pastoral
fellowships are declaring that unity without a mission is not
enough; and that the mission to be pursued is the fulfillment of
the Great Commission in our generation, beginning with the
city. I dare say that this battle, though not yet won, is well on its
way to being resolved.

So what is the devil up to now? He is trying to deceive pastors into carrying out the newly embraced mission individually
rather than in a united, coordinated thrust. This is where the
battle lines are drawn today.

Together and in One Accord

Now that prayer evangelism and lighthouses of prayer are being
embraced by the Church, and pastors have become familiar with
the concept, they need to do it together. Pastors of a city may be
in one accord as far as unity and mission is concerned, but if
they do not work together in a coordinated effort, what they will
get is piecemeal implementation at a much lower level of effectiveness than what God desires.

On the day of Pentecost the disciples were together and in
one accord (see Acts 2:1). Again, these are two complementary
but different things. The word "accord" refers to consensus,
while "together" speaks of physical proximity. It is possible to be
in one accord without being physically together; but it is impossible to do something together without being physically present.

This is the last frontier to be settled. The Church in the city
that is walking in unity needs to work together. To that effect,

we have found the weeklong, radio-driven strategy to be most helpful since it conveys to believers all over the city the sense of unity and mission the pastors have cultivated in their gatherings. This strategy also serves to establish outposts of love and concern for the lost all over town. Until a better strategy is found and tested, I cannot recommend strongly enough this weeklong thrust.

Trouble on Planet Earth

This is why we need to understand a biblical principle related to communication as revealed in Genesis 11. This is a very interesting passage that shows that God is concerned by the possibility of ungodly men attaining a level of power capable of posing a threat to His plans. That much is reflected in His statement: "This is what they began to do, and now nothing which they purpose to do will be impossible for them" (Gen. 11:6). This is quite a certification of extraordinary potential coming from One who Himself has unlimited potential. So who were these men and what were they were doing?

They were the descendants of Noah who settled on the plains of Shinar and made a covenant to do four things together: (1) to build a city, (2) to erect a tower to reach heaven, (3) to obtain a name for themselves and (4) to *not* go to the ends of the earth (see Gen. 11:1-4). These four objectives, inoffensive as they appear on the surface, belie a diabolic design, as they are the opposite of what God intends for us:

1. We are not to build a city on our own initiative but, rather, wait for the city whose builder and architect is God (see Heb. 11:10).

2. We have no need to try to reach heaven since the best of heaven came down to reach us (see John. 3:16).
3. We do not need to be known by our own names because there is no other name greater than the name of Jesus, the Lord of all (see Acts 4:12).
4. We are to go to the ends of the earth (see Matt. 28:19,20).

Because of their fourfold opposition to the will of God, we can easily discern Satan's machinations among the men of Shinar.

Now, let us discern why they posed such a threat. What were they doing? They were not building nuclear bombs or developing weapons of chemical warfare. They were baking bricks and gluing them with tar. So what causes the Trinity to intervene, lest they become unstoppable? The answer is in God's assessment of the people:

Behold, they are one people, and they all have the same language. And this is what they began to do, and now *nothing which they purpose to do will be impossible to them* (Gen.11:6, emphasis added).

God lists here three factors that, once combined, have the potential to render these men unstoppable:

1. A compelling, unifying *goal*: "This is what they began to do." They were not building walls in their spare time; they were building a city. And to accomplish this, they had settled down and agreed to dwell together.
2. They had *unity*: "They are one people."
3. They had *communication*: "They all have the same language."

The Unstoppable Formula

God was saying that when a group of people has a compelling purpose, unity and communication, *nothing is impossible for them*. This is not the hype of an enthusiastic evangelist; it is God's assessment! This is a very serious and important matter that deserves closer scrutiny. It wasn't what they were doing but *how* they were doing it—the combination of purpose, unity and communication—that produced unlimited potential.

Consider the implications for city-reaching efforts. If God Almighty somehow becomes concerned when a group of desperados, covered with mud and tar, tap into these three components, how much more is Satan and hell itself threatened right now by the prospect of pastors doing the same to reach their cities!

Remember:

Purpose + Unity + Communication = Unlimited Potential

Which one of the three components did God choose to disable among the men of Shinar? Communication! Why? Because if communication breaks down, the other two soon dissolve; hence the importance of moving a city-reaching initiative past unity and mission to *communication*. To do this, it is necessary for pastors to dwell together since sustainable communication depends on it.

On a practical level, this is what the weeklong prayer evangelism thrust accomplishes. The united citywide service on Sunday, the three radio broadcasts and the Saturday prayer fair use programmatic unity to communicate a compelling objective to the whole Church in the city. In chapter 9, we will look at specific suggestions for doing this. In the meantime, it should suffice to say that this weeklong thrust must always be the culmination and not the beginning of a process. Here are some key components that must precede the weeklong thrust:

- Weekly prayer and intercessory meetings of pastors and city elders (anything short of weekly meetings will not meet the criteria for togetherness)
- Reconciliation and restitution through identificational repentance
- Pulpit exchanges
- Celebrations of unity
- Weekly radio program devoted to prayer evangelism
- Gatherings of youth and intercessors

These activities have the potential to contribute to both the foundation and the focus for a process aimed at changing the spiritual climate over the city and eventually the region.

The Small City That Touched a Big State

In April 1999, a group of pastors in State College, Pennsylvania, led by Dan Nold, Paul Grabill, Mitch Smith and Sheng Tung Wu, decided to go for it and launched an initiative to reach their city. At first things did not look very promising, especially when one considers the small number of pastors willing to go the distance. Nevertheless, sensing that God was in it, they invited us to hold a City Reachers School in combination with a three-day radio launch of lighthouses of prayer. Even this was not a firm possibility, since the local radio station was not fully convinced it should participate.

Six weeks before the event, Jack Serra of Harvest Evangelism and the pastors of State College convened a statewide meeting for leaders interested in city reaching, and 320 people showed up.[5] More importantly, God showed up and everybody went home convinced that this initiative was God's idea.

Next, intercession was called in. Enter Barbara Knight. She organized prayer in the air, on water and on land. Twenty-three airplanes with intercessors on board flew over the state, covering Pennsylvania with prayer. Similar efforts were undertaken using boats and cars. Soon the entire state had been prayed for on site.

When the moment came to pre-record the radio broadcast— something the radio station requested we do in advance so that its board could review and approve the program—God raised the ante dramatically. While we were recording the programs, the station manager, Mark Vanouse, was deeply touched and suggested that we make the tapes available to other stations in the state. The response was extraordinary, to say the least. Twenty-two radio stations joined in and established an informal network that covered the entire state of Pennsylvania. In addition, Cornerstone TV provided three one-hour broadcasts scheduled for the same days as the radio broadcasts, producing a one-two media punch. Last but not least, close to a thousand leaders attended the City Reachers School—so many that the venue had to be moved from a church building to a secular hall.

The result was improvement of the spiritual climate statewide and renewed faith and vision for reaching cities and towns for Christ now! It caused the beginning of a youth revival and laid a foundation for Light the Nation, a major broadcast that six months later helped launch lighthouses of prayer in all 50 states.

Today, statewide prayer evangelism initiatives are popping up all over the country; but none of them was on the radar until the pastors in State College decided to go statewide. What they did constituted a powerful prophetic act. That, coupled with the impetus coming from the paradigm shifts already in place, helped to make a national city-reaching movement inevitable.

Yes, it is possible to change the spiritual climate over a city and region. The challenge then lies in sustaining that climate, and we will deal with that later. In the meantime, go for it. Sail with the tide. It is a powerful one!

Notes

1. The mission of the Church is to reach the lost—hence, the choosing of the moment when the first converts were made as the time of birth.
2. Richard Gatowski, *Just Add Water* (San Francisco: Voice of Pentecost, 1992), pp. 116, 117.
3. Rick Heeren is the vice president for Harvest Evangelism in the northern and central regions.
4. The Alpha Course, a discipleship program for seekers, was designed by Holy Trinity Anglican Church in Bronston, London.
5. Jack Serra is the vice president for Harvest Evangelism in the eastern region.

7

Emerging Paradigms

Dawn never bursts in, but emerges gently and gradually and its path is irreversible. So it is with these emerging paradigms.

Let us take a moment to connect the nine paradigms we have discussed into a single paragraph that will allow us to visualize the tremendous potential they contain for our city.

Picture one Church in the city, united and fully persuaded that the city can and must be reached for Christ now, mobilizing its members to conduct prayer evangelism without divisions because of identificational repentance. Imagine church services taking place all over town and public prayers being offered everywhere for everybody because pastors no longer restrict themselves to caring for the fold but are leading their parishioners to focus on the flock at large, the city. As a result, the spiritual climate over the city is being transformed into one of godliness.

The truth reflected by these nine paradigms no longer has to be argued; the Church is well on its way to being transformed by these changes in ways of doing ministry. The next four paradigms are already on the threshold and moving in on our consciousness. Dawn never bursts in but emerges gently and gradually and its path is irreversible. So it is with these emerging paradigms.

Paradigm #10:
Intercession Is a Spiritual Gift, But It Is Also Something All Christians Must Do

With all prayer and petition pray at all times in the Spirit, and with this in view, be on the alert with all perseverance and petition for all the saints (Eph. 6:18).

Intercession is a powerful and much-needed spiritual gift; but we have tended to see intercessors as something of a mystery, a puzzle to the rest of us. As their role became more recognized, we categorized these gifted prayer warriors as people who were highly unique and impossible to emulate. There is no question that they are uniquely gifted; but stopping there leads us to confine the practice of intercessory prayer to a select few when, in fact, it is something that every believer must be involved in, whether or not they are gifted in this area.

According to 1 Timothy 2:1-8, the *whole* Church is instructed to pray for everybody, everywhere. In 1 Thessalonians 5:17, we are all commanded to "pray without ceasing." In Ephesians 6:18, all the saints are told to pray at all times:

With *all* prayer and petition pray at *all* times in the Spirit, and with this in view, be on the alert with *all* perseverance and petition for *all* the saints (emphasis added).

The all-inclusive nature of this instruction indicates that prayer shouldn't be a condiment but the main dish in the Church's diet. Though there are different levels and scopes of intercession, everyone is called to intercede *at all times!*

Why is it important to understand that *everybody* can and should intercede? Because if we got this far with just a few intercessors praying, consider how much farther (and faster) we will get when *everyone* intercedes. Intercession is the midwife that delivers the Church's babies. Everything extraordinary that has happened in the last 10 years was birthed in a context attended by intercession.

Cindy Jacobs is the first top-level intercessor my wife, Ruth, and I ever met. Doris Wagner brought Cindy to Argentina at the beginning of the 1990 outreach in Resistencia. A couple of months later, Cindy and Doris led intercession for the nation in Plaza de Mayo in downtown Buenos Aires. We issued a nationwide call for intercessors, and a handful of about 50 showed up. Directed by Cindy, they did a superb job, praying for every government building that surrounds the plaza. They conducted identificational repentance and performed some prophetic acts. But they were still only a small group.

In November 1999, during a two-hour televised intercession meeting, thousands of intercessors gathered to pray in the same plaza and many more all over the nation. As the secular saying goes, "You've come a long way, baby!"

Intercession Goes Mainstream
Since 1990, intercession has become an integral part of the life of the Church—so much so that intercessors praying on site is

now considered an indispensable part of Church activities in the field. George Otis, Jr.'s recent book *Informed Intercession* (Renew Books) has taken the strategic dimension of intercession to new heights. Today, few in the Church would even think about undertaking a major initiative without a prayer shield in place. Bill Bright does it with his fasting and prayer gatherings. Promise Keepers has a full-time paid position for a director of prayer, whose main job is to pray at the headquarters and to coordinate intercession at all P.K. events. Our son-in-law, Gary Arneson, filled that position for a while and told us how much Coach Bill McCartney depends on intercessory prayer.

Until recently, intercession was thought to be the job of a few highly gifted and perceptive people only. This is now evolving into a widespread belief that intercession is something everybody should do. I went through this transition myself after reading C. Peter Wagner's book *Prayer Shield* (Regal Books). My wife, Ruth, is an intercessor, but we both saw the need for additional intercessory covering for our family and our ministry. God soon led Ted and Sandra Hahs to covenant with us to provide our prayer shield. Ted was in Resistencia with us in 1990 when the city was reached. He later married Sandra, a ballerina with the National Ballet of Portugal. Both of them are what Wagner calls "I-1" intercessors—the top level.

When Ted and Sandra began joining us on ministry trips, I was touched by their devotion to prayer. They would pray for hours, fast for days and stay up all night interceding in prayer. After a while, I found myself expanding my prayer life; I was surprised at how easily I could pray for two, three, even four hours! I discovered an intercessory dimension in me I did not know I had. Soon we were renting additional office space to establish an intercessory chapel at Harvest Evangelism headquarters, and everybody's job description was rewritten. Now each staff member is listed as an intercessor who just happens to do a certain job.

Children Intercessors?

Perhaps the most dramatic development in prayer in recent years has been the emergence of children as intercessors. These are children who hear from God, see angels, receive words from the Holy Spirit and lay hands on the sick and see them healed. During our fall conference in Argentina for the International Institute on Prayer Evangelism (IIPE), we take the participants to experience church meetings run by children, ages 3 to 11. These young ones open the meeting, lead worship, preach and do all-out intercession. They have also led the congregation on a prayer expedition through the neighborhood and have organized a mini prayer fair to pray for the felt needs of the lost.

Focus on the Arrows, Not the Quiver

Why should children intercede? Why not? Paul exhorts *all* the saints to pray (Eph. 6:18) and children are saints, too. In Psalm 127, a psalm dealing with city reaching, we are told that the house (home) will be built and the city protected by the Lord who "gives to His beloved even in his sleep" (v. 2)—a reference to God's provision for the house and the city to be secure. What is God's provision? The answer is in the next verse: "Children are a gift of the LORD" (v. 3). It is important not to miss the connection between these two verses because it shows that God gives children to us in order to help build the house and protect the city. This is quite a new paradigm, as the Church has never looked to children as helpers, much less important helpers, in city reaching. But this is what it says:

Like arrows in the hand of a warrior, so are the children of one's youth. How blessed is the man whose quiver is full of them (Ps. 127:4,5).

Until now we have seen children as weak and needy, and our efforts have been geared toward protecting rather than recruiting them. But in this passage children are presented as weapons in our hands, poised for war, ready to inflict damage on the adversary. This means that we need to stop protecting the arrows in our quiver and, instead, pull them out and point them at the enemy.

WE NEED TO STOP PROTECTING THE ARROWS IN OUR QUIVER AND, INSTEAD, PULL THEM OUT AND POINT THEM AT THE ENEMY.

Any soldier/archer who makes protecting the arrows in his quiver the primary objective will be hurt and his arrows scattered. Unfortunately, this is exactly what we have done with children as far as ministry is concerned. It is high time the Church tap into this resource for ministry. Then "they shall not be ashamed, when they speak with their enemies in the gate" (Ps. 127:5).

Please notice the transition from "he" in verse 4, the warrior with arrows in his hand, to "they" in verse 5. Who are "they"? They are the warrior and his children, united in battle against the enemy. Furthermore, notice that neither the house nor the city are threatened anymore because they are holding the enemy back at the gate. What gate? The gate of the city, because this is as far as the arrow can fly.

Here are five reasons why children make *superior* intercessors:

1. They see God because they are pure in heart (see Matt. 5:8).
2. They have angels assigned to them, making them familiar with angelic ministry. Many children have seen angels, whereas most adults are not sure angels are *supposed* to be around them (see Matt. 18:10).
3. They believe God when He speaks to them. Most adults believe *in* God but do not believe Him when He speaks to them (see Matt. 18:3-5).
4. They are much more difficult targets for the accuser of the brethren. When it comes to accusing me, the devil has a library full of files from which to draw. When it comes to my grandchildren, what can he accuse them of? That they did not brush their teeth properly or that they spilled their milk? Their purity makes them unstoppable arrows (see 1 Cor. 14:20)!
5. Children are naturally attracted to Jesus (see Mark 10:15).

Children are natural-born intercessors, and it is far better to release them while they are children, so that they can develop a lifestyle of intercession. I believe God is releasing children into intercession to convince us adults that intercession is something everybody should do.

The Need for Reconciliation

In the early 1990s when intercession was beginning to emerge in America, not much was going on in the San Francisco Bay area. We talked to pastors who told us what they saw was wrong among intercessors: weak marriages, dysfunctional families, emotional instability and "sugar-coated" prophecies—meaning they never said anything negative to those to whom they ministered. We then talked to intercessors who shared how much they had been wounded and despised by pastors. We soon realized that not much would be accomplished until this breach was repaired. This led to A Day for Intercessors, a one-day event held on the north, south, east and west sides of the bay. Pastors and intercessors from the area were invited to participate.

We opened the meeting with a biblical perspective on intercession and a survey of the ministry minefield that needed to be deactivated. We cautioned the intercessors that each mine was an excess or mistake on their part that pastors have complained about. We explained to the pastors that the very issues they have used to disqualify intercessors are the ones that made them intercessors in the first place. Domestic problems or childhood traumas drove them closer to God out of desperation, and they were now learning how to overcome these injuries through intercession.

It was also helpful for pastors to hear that what some considered to be sugar-coated words from the Lord were indeed genuine words of affirmation. We explained to them how intercessors cannot hold anything against those for whom they are interceding because doing so would invalidate their role as intercessors (see 1 Pet. 4:7-10).

We then turned the meeting over to pastors and intercessors who shared from their hearts, leading to repentance and reconciliation between both groups. The powerful event climaxed with Communion and the commissioning of intercessors by their pastors.

Intercession Around the Bay

Intercession around the bay has continued to increase. Susan Bagley founded Revival Strategies International to pray for each pastor in the Bay Area. Pat Chen of First Love Ministries contributes greatly to the existing canopy of prayer over the area by mobilizing intercessors. Lillian Poon established IHOP (International House of Prayer) in the South Bay. Valley Christian School, the largest in Santa Clara County, has incorporated intercession into its daily routine. They even offer a course on prayer evangelism!

In the Bay Area the validity of intercession is no longer questioned, nor is it limited to a few intercessors. I suggest that if there isn't a strong prayer shield over your city or region, you begin by facilitating reconciliation between pastors and intercessors. This will soon result in the spread of intercession. Imagine how much better things will be when all the saints in your area pray at all times!

Paradigm #11:
Martyrdom Is a Possibility on Standby for All Christians

And they overcame him because of the blood of the Lamb and because of the word of their testimony, and they did not love their life even to death (Rev. 12:11).

Since our struggle is against the devil and his forces of wickedness (see Eph. 6:10-18), it is of paramount importance that we know *how* to defeat him. Revelation 12:11 spells out the formula, which consists of three parts: the blood of the Lamb, the word of our testimony and our willingness to die for what we believe. These three components must be brought to bear in order for victory to happen.

We have no problem accessing the blood of Jesus, since He shed it once and for all on the cross. Speaking the word of our testimony is something we are learning to do with greater boldness. The real challenge lies in the third component, as it involves the possibility of death—our death.

There is a natural reluctance we all share when it comes to the subject of death. When death is contemplated as a result of a battle the prospect becomes even less appealing, since to the ugliness traditionally associated with death we now add the prospect of pain and suffering. Nevertheless, without this third component in place, unless we are willing to die for the Lord, the formula will not work. This brings up the subject of martyrdom.

A Possibility on Standby for All

If martyrdom is a spiritual gift, it is a gift that can be exercised only once because the moment we do it we are dead! Nevertheless, our attitudes towards martyrdom are beginning to change. The courageous deaths of several teenage Christians in recent school shootings in America have driven home the message of Revelation 12:11 in a hard-to-ignore way. We need to overcome our fear of death if we are to overcome the ultimate enemy, Satan.

Fear of death is one of the most paralyzing fears. Worse yet, it is an enslaving fear. In Hebrews 2:14,15 we are told that the devil holds people captive all their lives through the fear of death—a life sentence! The enemy knows that as long as we are afraid of death, we will lack the boldness necessary to struggle successfully against the forces of evil (see Eph. 6:19,20). Such fear causes us to value our earthly lives too highly and prevents us from being effective spiritual warriors.

To give you an idea how much we are affected by this fear, consider this: What is the most commonly asked question about the Great Tribulation and the Antichrist? "Will we as Christians have to go through the tribulation? Will we have to face the Antichrist?" This fear has produced distorted teachings and bland theology that are useless when it comes to dealing with pain, poverty, suffering and tribulations.

The Death of Christians Is Beautiful

Christians need to realize that dying for the Lord is a blessing: "Precious in the sight of the LORD is the death of His godly ones" (Ps.116:15). Such a death is precious because it brings about the moment when the Lord replaces our tattered tent with a home on the best real estate, heaven (see 2 Cor. 5:1). The moment this truth is fully understood, Christians will cease to be controlled by the fear of death. They will be able to welcome the hardships and the sufferings necessary to see the kingdom of God established on Earth.

This is why the paradigm shift that presents martyrdom as a possibility on standby for *all* Christians holds so much promise. A successful soldier is one who knows *how* to fight, is *willing* to fight and fights *to the finish*. Such a soldier is a superior warrior, and a squad of this kind of spiritual commandos makes for a formidable fighting force.

Die Beforehand, So You Don't Have to Die Later

When a military mission has a less than 50 percent chance of success, it is considered to be a suicide mission. After fully explaining the risks involved, the officer in charge asks for volunteers to take a step forward. When a commando does so, the moment he sets his foot down, death ceases to be a factor in the equation as far as he is concerned because, emotionally, he died when he stepped forward. Now he is as good as dead and,

EVERY PERSON IN THE CHURCH MUST BE WILLING AND EAGER TO LAY DOWN HIS LIFE FOR JESUS. NOTHING MAKES A WELL-EQUIPPED ARMY MIGHTIER THAN FEARLESSNESS!

consequently, fear of death will not distract or occupy him anymore. This attitude can turn the odds in his favor, because his target most likely will be concerned with safeguarding his own life. The commando's lack of preoccupation gives him a decisive edge and, more often than not, it allows him to come back alive from the suicide mission.

Why is this paradigm important? Because the blood of martyrs always produces an extraordinary harvest of souls, as seen throughout history. If Stephen's martyrdom resulted in the tremendous expansion of Christianity (see Acts 11:19-21), how much more will happen when every person in the Church is willing and even eager to lay down his or her life for Jesus? The Church in the Third World has a lot to offer in this area. Persecution, tribulations and torture have purified and strengthened the faith of its members. God has moved many of these members to the United States and to Western Europe. They are rich in faith. They know how to walk across the threshold leading to this new paradigm. When the rest of us cross this same threshold, we will become a Church that is fearless, and nothing makes a well-equipped army mightier than fearlessness!

Paradigm #12:
All the Offices of Ephesians 4
Need Restoration

> Walk in a manner worthy of the calling with which you
> have been called. He gave some as apostles, and some as
> prophets, and some as evangelists, and some as pastors
> and teachers, for the equipping of the saints (Eph.
> 4:1,11,12).

There is a growing consensus that the prophetic ministry was in
need of restoration and that this restoration began in the 1980s.
Subsequently, the 1990s became a decade of restoration to the
Church of the apostolic ministry. Quite a bit of thinking, writing and dialogue has been generated regarding the offices of
apostle and prophet in recent years and, as a result, a better
understanding of the issues involved in the nature and the func-
tion of these two offices is emerging, even though in some circles
the subject remains controversial.

C. Peter Wagner has, as usual, provided leadership in this
arena by creating forums where these issues are addressed
intelligently, without prejudice and, above all, combining biblical scholarship with substantive field research. His books
Churchquake (Regal Books) and *Apostles of the City* (Wagner
Leadership Institute) are absolutely must reads on this subject.

Unfortunately, we have assumed that the other offices mentioned in Ephesians 4—pastors, evangelists and teachers—are not
in need of restoration, based on the assumption that what we
have today (and have had for hundreds of years) conforms to
biblical standards. However, a careful study of Ephesians 4 presents a different picture.

In the popular mind, an evangelist is a person endowed with charismatic gifts and above-average communication skills who packs stadiums and preaches to multitudes or who enthusiastically and faithfully witnesses to sinners in bus stations and on sidewalks. Those are valid and absolutely necessary expressions of evangelism. However, an evangelist, as described in Ephesians 4, is someone who equips the saints so that *the saints* do the work of the ministry (of evangelism). This person is meant to be an equipper who enables the Church to do the job, not someone who does it *for* the Church.

Likewise, a pastor is not supposed to watch over believers, ignoring the lost until they have joined his congregation. Rather, he is to copastor the city with other undershepherds because the lost are as much his responsibility as are the saints. To reach the lost multitudes, he must make it one of his highest priorities to equip his members to shepherd the people in their circle of influence.

Similarly, a teacher is called to use his knowledge of doctrine and history to build up all the saints and show them how to major on the majors rather than on the minors. His lectures and books should always aim at speaking or writing the truth in love to help the Church grow in all aspects into Christ, "from whom *the whole body*, being fitted and held together by that which every joint supplies, according to the proper working of each individual part, causes the growth of the body for the building up of itself in love" (Eph. 4:16, emphasis added). Paul Cedar, Francis Schaeffer, James Dobson, Ted Haggard, Larry Jackson, Jay Swallow, Bill Bright, Francis Frangipane, Mark Pollard, Dick Eastman, Dave Bryant and many others like them fit into this category. Sitting under their teaching always produces a deeper appreciation of the Church and its diversity and a stronger longing for knowing more of and about Jesus.

This paradigm shift is crucial because unless we see the need to have the offices of evangelist, pastor and teacher restored to sound biblical standards, the current structure will not be able to assimilate the end-time harvest and, consequently, our cities will not be reached. This will come into sharper focus when we look at the next emerging paradigm.

Paradigm #13: Loving the Lost Is as Essential As Loving God

"YOU SHALL LOVE THE LORD YOUR GOD WITH ALL YOUR HEART, AND WITH ALL YOUR SOUL, AND WITH ALL YOUR MIND." This is the great and foremost commandment. The second is like it, "YOU SHALL LOVE YOUR NEIGHBOR AS YOURSELF." On these two commandments depend the whole Law and the Prophets. (Matt. 22:37-40).

Have you ever wondered why many of the recent sparks of revival around the world have attracted lots of saints but few sinners? Isn't it logical to expect that sinners would be drawn to the tangible presence of the One who loves them and who delivered Himself to be slain for them?

Sinners are not drawn to these events because we in the Church have embraced a serious misconception: that the closer we get to God, the farther we must be from sinners. We have a distorted idea of revival that emphasizes our relationship with God at the expense of our relationship with the lost. *There is no biblical basis for this position.*

One of the reasons why it is so easy to succumb to this dichotomy is because it sounds so pious, loving God and shunning sinners. I have asked several people who have a passion for revival and who are either praying for or enjoying it, "What is revival like?" Their usual reply is something like, "The presence and the glory of God flooding our souls; praise and worship filling the air; holiness oxygenating our spirits." I ask, "Is that all?" "Isn't the glory and the presence of God, holiness, praise and worship enough?" they retort.

Not really. If all we want is the glory and the presence of God in an atmosphere of holiness, praise and worship, we should pray for a heart attack, drop dead and go to heaven! Then we will enjoy all those wonderful manifestations immediately and forever.

Those majestic, wonderful manifestations are extremely important and absolutely necessary, but they constitute only the first wave of revival. God bestows them on us to make us more like Jesus. But once we become like Him, we must seek those whom *He* came to seek and save. Consequently, the ultimate expression of revival should be multitudes of sinners coming to Jesus.

It Takes Two Commandments

It is of paramount importance to understand that we cannot say we love God, whom we cannot see, if we do not love our neighbor, whom we constantly see (see 1 John 4:20). These two loves and the commandments that mandate them cannot be separated, since the source of love for both is the same: God's love. We love God because He first loved us and left a deposit of love in us that we can use to love Him (see 1 John 4:19). Likewise, we are incapable of loving our neighbors as ourselves on our own, but the love of God in us allows us to do it.

When Jesus quoted the greatest commandment, to love God, He made a point of presenting it alongside the second greatest commandment, to love our neighbor. These commands are interconnected and presented as integral parts of each other. Jesus taught in no uncertain terms that we must love God *and* love our neighbor as ourselves.

One Hundred Percent Response to the Gospel

I was pointed in the direction of this paradigm while trying to understand a sweeping statement found in Luke 16:16: "The Law and the prophets were proclaimed until John; since then the gospel of the kingdom of God is preached, and everyone is forcing his way into it." Jesus said that *everyone* was *forcing* his way into the Kingdom. Why is it that today hardly anyone wishes to come to church, much less force his or her way into it?

At first I reasoned that it was because the Church preaches the Law and the prophets instead of the gospel of the kingdom of God. This sounded cool and imaginative, but it isn't the case, and the Lord soon rebuked me. He told me not to knock the Law and the prophets, since every time I open the Bible I am looking at them. Besides, Jesus did not come to put down or abrogate either one but to fulfill both.

When I asked the Lord what Luke 16:16 meant then, He showed me this structural picture of the verse: the proclamation of the Law and the prophets created a foundation, a platform upon which the gospel of the kingdom of God is preached. So appealing is this gospel that listeners force their way in. But the key to getting such a response is not the gospel being preached but the *foundation* on which it is preached, that is the Law and the prophets, because everybody welcomes and loves to hear good news. Today, the Church preaches the same good news, the gospel, but the lost do not receive it. Why? Because the Church does not use the same foundation described in Luke 16:16.

After showing me the structural blueprint of this passage, the Lord directed me to Matthew 22:34-40, where the Law and the prophets are discussed further. A religious teacher asked Jesus a loaded question in an attempt to trick Him: "Teacher, which is the great commandment in the Law?" (v. 36). He wanted Jesus to highlight only one commandment. Instead, after quoting the greatest commandment, Jesus added, quite emphatically, "The second is like it, 'YOU SHALL LOVE YOUR NEIGHBOR AS YOURSELF'" (v. 39).

To stress that these commandments cannot be separated from each other, He said, "On these *two* commandments depend the *whole* Law and the prophets" (v. 40, emphasis added). Please, do not miss Jesus' main point: In order to fulfill the Law and the prophets—that is, the heart of the Scriptures—it is not enough to love God. We also need to love our neighbor as ourselves.

The reason why multitudes do not respond to the gospel we preach is that even though we love God, we do not love them as much as we love ourselves, and that contaminates the message.

Jesus' Frustration and Jesus' Exhilaration

There is a biblical precedent for this in the Gospel of Luke. In chapter 9, Jesus reached what perhaps was His lowest emotional point, and He scolded His disciples: "O unbelieving and perverted generation, how long shall I be with you, and put up with you?" (v. 41). He addressed those strong words not to the Pharisees or the scribes, but to His own apostles! Clearly, He was very upset and tempted with overwhelming discouragement.

Yet soon after, in Luke 10, Jesus reached a pinnacle of joy: "At that very time He rejoiced greatly in the Holy Spirit" (v. 21). This was no small joy. He was overflowing with it! What a contrast between His exhilaration here and His frustration displayed in the previous chapter.

What caused Jesus to experience emotions so radically different? The outcome of spiritual warfare! Earlier, a demon defeated His disciples (see Luke 9:40). Later, His disciples beat every demon they came across, and even the devil fell down (Luke 10:17,18). When the devil beat His disciples, Jesus became discouraged; but when His disciples beat the devil, He was very encouraged indeed.

There is also a human factor at work here that should not be overlooked. Jesus worked with two different sets of disciples: the Twelve, who were defeated in chapter 9, and the so-called Seventy, who proved victorious in chapter 10. Both groups loved Jesus; but the Twelve resented sinners, while the Seventy seemed to enjoy their company. The contrast between these groups provides the key to the paradigm under discussion.

A quick look at the series of events in Luke 9 shows how the Twelve displayed the following characteristics, evidence of their resentment of the multitude:

- *Self-centered.* "And when the Apostles returned, they gave an account to Him *of all that they had done*" (v. 10, emphasis added). Note how self-focused their report is compared to that of the Seventy, who later returned with joy because of the good things that had happened for demonized people.

- *Uncaring.* Jesus took the Twelve on a spiritual retreat. I am sure they were pleased with this opportunity to be alone with Jesus. But the multitude followed. Jesus' response to this interruption was very positive: "Welcoming them, He began speaking to them . . . and curing those who had need of healing" (v. 11). The Twelve, on the other hand, were very negative: "Send the multitude away" (v. 12).

- *Haughty.* Jesus was not pleased with their uncaring attitude and told them to give them something to eat (see v. 13). The disciples demurred, so Jesus commanded them, "Have them recline to eat in groups of about fifty each" (v. 14). I suspect He had the Twelve organize the multitude in groups to force them to come in close contact with the people. Otherwise, they may have simply shouted at the hungry people, "Sit down!"

- *Spiteful.* When Jesus asked the Twelve who the multitudes believed He was (see v. 18), I imagine the apostles felt very superior, since they had a pretty good idea who Jesus was, whereas the multitudes had flunked Theology 101.

- *Unworthy messengers.* I wonder what their faces registered when "He warned them, and instructed them not to tell this (that He was the Christ of God) to anyone" (v. 21). Why would Jesus prohibit His apostles from preaching such a powerful truth? The answer is found two verses down: "If anyone wishes to come after Me, let him deny himself, and take up his cross daily, and follow Me" (v. 23). They were not ready to meet this criteria, especially the last one, to follow

Him. Jesus was more than eager to go where sinners were and to welcome them when they descended unannounced on Him, whereas the Twelve wanted them dismissed. Jesus did not want preachers who correctly preached the truth but misrepresented His character before his friends, the sinners.

- *Confused.* Jesus took the three leaders—Peter, James and John—to a mountaintop retreat. The moment they saw "His glory" (v. 32), Peter, not knowing what he was saying (meaning that he was not in control of what he was saying), blurted out, "It is good for us to be here; and let us make three tabernacles" (v. 33). This was so out of order that God the Father rebuked Peter and commanded him in no uncertain terms to keep quiet (see vv. 34,35).

- *Greedy.* Peter's motivation to do something for Jesus and His guests was the lowest: "It is good for us." Choosing to ignore the multitude waiting in the valley, Peter and the other two were thinking only of what was good for themselves.

- *Powerless.* When the four came down from the mountain, a local man outlined two problems for Jesus. The first one was his: He had a son who was brutally tormented by demons. The second problem was Jesus': "I begged Your disciples to cast it out, and they could not" (v. 40). It is at this point that Jesus hit rock bottom and indicted His disciples, labeling them perverted and unbelieving. At first this seems like an overreaction, especially in light of the fact that the demon was cast out right away by Him. However, when the disciples inquired why they had failed, Jesus told them that it was for lack of faith. He then explained that this particular kind of demon came out only by fasting (see Matt. 17:19-22). It seems the disciples were willing to go through the abstract motions of ministry but were unwilling to deny themselves, as required by fasting, for the benefit of such an unappealing case.

- *Proud.* "An argument arose among them as to which of them might be the greatest" (v. 46). This is as ridiculous as if the players on a football team who had lost their last 40 games got into a nasty locker-room fight over who among them was the team MVP!

- *Controlling.* They found someone who was doing what they failed to do—casting out demons—and they hindered him "because he does not follow along with us" (v. 49).

- *Delusional.* They had not been able to do a single thing right, but they felt very confident they could command God, of all people, to send fire from heaven (see v. 54).

- *Unmerciful.* They wished to see the Samaritans consumed by fire. This caused Jesus to observe that they were working for the devil rather than for Him (see v. 55).

Please do not miss the next observation. It is perplexing that the Twelve were capable of being selfish, uncaring, haughty, spiteful, unworthy spokespersons, confused, greedy, inefficient, proud, controlling, delusional and unmerciful and still love Jesus. How can that be? *Because they embraced the mistaken belief that in order to be close to Jesus, it is necessary to stay away from sinners.*

Jesus Changes Teams

In chapter 10, Jesus got a new set of disciples. We are not told their names and we are not sure if they numbered 70 or 72. I believe that this vagueness as to their biographies and exact number is intentional on the part of the Holy Spirit to emphasize that the key is neither their quantity or personal credentials but their obedience. Obedience means getting out of the barn and going where the harvest is. To make sure that this most important principle was not lost with His new team, Jesus spelled out a detailed, outward-facing strategy: *Go, bless, fellowship, meet needs and proclaim.*

Today, we have a clear choice: We can be like the Twelve or like the Seventy. The former caused great pain to Jesus, the latter great joy. Jesus called the Twelve perverted and unbelieving, and there was good reason for this. They were perverted because they had deviated from the original design to serve others and were serving only themselves. They were unbelieving because they chose not to believe that Jesus came to save rather than to destroy sinners.

When we allow our love for God to be pitted against the need to love the lost, we find the prospect of resenting sinners very appealing. Nothing could be farther from the heart of God and from the Scriptures. We need to do both simultaneously and in harmony. If we don't, we will pervert our purpose and will deny Jesus' main reason for coming to earth. This is serious!

Are We Perverted and Unbelieving?

If the bulk of our budget goes to minister to saints rather than the lost, the Lord calls us perverted and unbelieving. If the majority of our time is spent away from the needy and the hurting (see Isaiah 58), the Lord calls us perverted and unbelieving. If we devote the bulk of our preaching to condemning the lost without feeling Jesus' pain for them, the Lord calls us perverted and unbelieving. If the motivation behind what we do for the

Lord is because it is good for us rather than for the lost, the Lord calls us perverted and unbelieving.

We cannot claim to love God if we do not love our neighbor. This dichotomy is the heart of the religious spirit that has controlled us for too long. To correct this, the Holy Spirit is communicating a clear and compelling message: Loving the lost is as essential as loving God if we are going to reach the sinners in our cities for Christ.

A Love Encounter With Gays

I see encouraging signs that this paradigm is beginning to emerge into the light of day. In November 1999, during our annual conference in Argentina, we scheduled a two-hour television broadcast live from Plaza de Mayo in Buenos Aires. Our objective was to pray for the lost and to bless the nation. As soon as we had obtained all the permits and published the event, the Argentine Coalition of Gays and Lesbians announced that they would stage a protest march in the same place and at the same time.

When I asked the Lord why He allowed this to happen—given the extreme potential for mishaps, violence, even hijacking of our meeting by the gays—the Lord said, "You planned a meeting to pray for sinners. I am sending you the best specimens."

When the day came, the gays and lesbians occupied the plaza while we were finishing up. They were loud and provocative; many were essentially naked. The decorations on their floats were rude and immoral. However, our team went to them and asked their forgiveness for the Church's rejection and anger towards them. The gays who saw this were perplexed and asked, "Who are you?" Our people responded that they were Christians. The gays retorted, "You are not Christians. Christians hate us."

We told them that such lack of love is what caused us to ask for their forgiveness. They were blown away.

Nevertheless, the gays and lesbians insisted on cutting through our crowd when their march began. The police advised us that they could stop them from doing so, but they could not prevent them from becoming violent. We told them not to bother. When the gays began to march toward us, I picked up the microphone and signaled for the loudspeakers to be given maximum volume. Then I directed our crowd to turn toward the floats of gays and lesbians marching through our space, and I led everybody in a corporate prayer for the gays.

It was a prayer evangelist's dream come true. A multitude of industrial-strength, duly certified sinners were walking through our public prayer meeting. When we repented for the ugly and malodorous sins of discrimination and hatred and asked God to heal those afflicted with AIDS, the gays and lesbians were deeply touched and some began to cry. A few of them left the parade, put clothes on and joined us, and nine of them received the Lord. The media was there in full force, anticipating a hateful confrontation. Instead, they saw the love of Jesus in action. The next day, the newspapers in Argentina carried the story and all of them were highly affirming of this different brand of Christians.

I submit to you that when we give a glass of water in His name, when we take care of the needy, when we set the captives free from economic bondage, we are lifting Jesus up. Jesus says, "And I, if I be lifted up from the earth, will draw all men to Myself" (John 12:32). How many people does Jesus assure us will be attracted to Him when He is lifted up? All! Our mission is to lift Him up, the rest will just happen: Everybody will be attracted to Him.

Sadly, we have restricted our understanding of what constitutes lifting Jesus up to the practice of preaching. What a contrast to the words of Saint Francis of Assisi, who said, "Preach at all times. Use words only if necessary."[1]

If They Can See Us, They Should See God Through Us

The love with which God loves us that in turn enables us to love Him back is the same love we already have in our hearts for our neighbors, albeit unused. We need to release it by faith. When we do so, we will see Luke 16:16 fulfilled: everyone forcing their way into the Kingdom.

Why would this appeal to everyone? Because when we love the lost with the same love with which we love God, they feel connected to God, whom they cannot see, through us, whom they see, and through our love, which they can feel. If this paradigm is in place, the lost will not be able to resist the gospel of the Kingdom we preach.

Let me combine these four emerging paradigms in a single paragraph to picture the near future of the Church in our city:

Everybody in the Church intercedes for the lost, battling against the devil who has blinded them. They do so without fear of death because they have despised their lives unto death. Led by evangelists who equip them to witness wherever they are, by pastors who shepherd the entire city and make no distinction between saints and sinners as far as commitment and care, and by teachers who expound on the Word of the Lord for the purpose of building up the Body of Christ, the Church constitutes a living parable of a community that loves God and its neighbors with utmost intensity, and the Lord adds daily to those who are being saved!

Note
1. Source unknown.

FUTURE PARADIGMS

These paradigms will signal the beginning of the much-prayed-for revival and the gathering of the end-time harvest.

The paradigms that are the essence of this chapter are not yet in place; but when the shift toward them comes, it will signal the beginning of the much-prayed-for revival—the greatest ever—and the gathering of the end-time harvest. These paradigms represent the continental divide the Church must cross to settle the last frontier and fulfill the Great Commission in every city on every continent.

Paradigm #14:
The Harvest Is Plentiful

The harvest is plentiful (Matt. 9:37).

Behold, I say to you, lift up your eyes, and look on the fields, that they are white for harvest (John 4:35).

Jesus told His disciples, "The harvest is plentiful, but the workers are few. Ask the Lord of the harvest, therefore, to send out workers into his harvest field" (Luke 10:2, *NIV*). This is one of the most misunderstood texts in the Bible.

Often when we read this passage or hear it quoted, we get a vague sense of uneasiness, of negativity. I see three reasons for this: (1) there seems to be a problem with the harvesters, which is true since Jesus says they are few and in the wrong place when there's work to be done; (2) God seems here to need our help—which is not true—to remind Him when and where to send His workers; and (3) a call to prayer, like the one in this passage, has always been associated with a crisis. These factors conspire to leave us with a negative impression.

However, this teaching of our Lord is anything but negative. In fact, it begins on an extremely upbeat note: "The harvest is plentiful." The most positive term a farmer can use to describe any harvest is "plentiful." A plentiful harvest reflects the successful combination of good seed, good planting, good soil and timely watering, resulting in a high yield. No harvest can be plentiful without all of these factors.

Harvesters Allergic to Wheat
A careful examination of the text indicates that Jesus' concern was not with the quantity of the harvest or with the quality of the Management. Instead, His concern was with the harvesters—they were in the wrong place, waiting inside and praying for a great harvest; meanwhile, outside there was a plentiful harvest waiting to be brought in. This is our problem today: We are allergic to wheat. We do not care to associate with the lost, so we hide in our barns, praying for a wind of revival powerful enough to uproot the wheat and *blow it into* the barn!

The solution? Move the harvesters into the harvest fields. If the harvesters get together with the harvest, something good is bound to happen—after all, they are made for each other—especially if the harvest is plentiful.

What we do not quite understand is just *how* plentiful is plentiful. We know there has to be more than what we have gathered thus far—but how *much* more? A survey of the Gospels reveals that the coming harvest is, in fact, quantifiable: Jesus gave every indication that a minimum of half of the population would be saved! For example, in His parable of the ten virgins, five are saved and five aren't (see Matt. 25:1-13). He told us about two men working in the field and two women grinding grain; in each case, one is taken and the other left behind (see Luke 17:35,36). Jesus Himself was crucified between two thieves. One believed that He was the Christ and was saved; the other refused and was not saved (see Luke 23:39-43).

At first, this estimate of a 50 percent yield seems to contrast with another well-known teaching of Jesus:

> Enter by the narrow gate; for the gate is wide, and the way is broad that leads to destruction, and many are those who enter by it. For the gate is small, and the way is narrow that leads to life, and few are those who find it (Matt. 7:13,14).

Doesn't Jesus tell us here that the harvest will be small? I don't believe so, for at least three reasons:

1. What Jesus is describing here is the natural difficulty that fallen people have finding the way that leads to life, hence the need for us to show it to them.

2. His comparison between gates—the narrow and the wide—is more a statement on man's fallen nature and his resulting tendency towards evil than a prediction that, ultimately, very few will be saved.

3. This verse is set in a context of warnings against false prophets who promise an easy but false way. As we have come to learn, grace is free, but access to it costs us everything.

Bigger *Is* Better: The Expanding Kingdom

The trend throughout the New Testament is toward an increase, not a decrease, in the size of the harvest. Jesus painted the lost as fields white unto harvest (see John 4:35). He was followed everywhere by a multitude who responded enthusiastically to His message, forcing their way into the Kingdom (see Luke 16:16). Little changed in the book of Acts, where we read of thousands coming to salvation, entire cities being filled with the doctrine of the apostles and everyone hearing the word of the Lord (see Acts 19:10).

In the first sermon ever preached in the Church age, Peter stated unequivocally that God was going to pour His Spirit upon *all* flesh and that whosoever calls on His name shall be saved (see Acts 2:14-36). All flesh means *all* flesh—the entire population of the world. It is reasonable to assume that most of those on whom God pours His Spirit will call on the name of the Lord, because we, as believers, know how disarming and how inviting His touch is. Even Saul the persecutor, who had Christian blood on his hands and was bent on a murderous assignment, could not resist Him (see Acts 9:5).

In the book of Revelation, John testifies that the multitude around the heavenly throne was so huge that it defied counting:

I looked, and behold, a great multitude, which no one could count, from every nation and all tribes and peoples and tongues, standing before the throne and before the Lamb . . . saying, "Salvation to our God who sits on the throne, and to the Lamb" (Rev. 7:9-11).

At the very end of the New Testament, we are told that all "the nations shall walk by [the] light [of the New Jerusalem], and the kings of the earth shall bring their glory into it" (Rev. 21:24). And so as to leave no room for speculation that these nations and kings are saved, John writes, "And nothing unclean and no one who practices abomination and lying, shall ever come into it, *but only those whose names are written in the Lamb's book of life*" (Rev. 21:27, emphasis added).

The New Testament shows God's kingdom always expanding, never shrinking. The Bible is not only clear that there will be a plentiful harvest; it is emphatic about it.

The Church Is a Movement, Not a Monument

When we finally realize how plentiful the harvest is, we will change the way we do church. The Church will cease to be a monument, confined to one place, to a physical structure, and it will become once again a dynamic movement that expresses itself daily all over the city. Imagine what your city would be like if a minimum of half of the city's residents accepted the salvation offered by Jesus Christ. Wouldn't that be wonderful? You may wonder, *Where would a church that size meet? Shouldn't we be thinking about enlarging our present buildings?* No. God already has those buildings in place. They are called sports arenas!

When the harvest comes, the Church will have no choice but to meet all over the city in homes, in shops, in parks. When we need to come together as a Church, those sports stadiums will come in handy. In fact, we could be "doing church" before and after every game, even at halftime if half of the fans are believers. Open your eyes and see the fields. They are white unto harvest, and it is a plentiful one!

Paradigm #15:
The Lord's Return as Motivation to Fulfill the Great Commission

Men of Galilee, why do you stand looking into the sky? This Jesus, who has been taken up from you into heaven, will come in just the same way as you have watched Him go into heaven (Acts 1:11).

Our motivation behind what we do determines (1) how we do it, (2) the scope of what we do and (3) how much we are willing to invest in the way of time, money and effort. The Early Church believed with a passion that Jesus was returning in their lifetime. Paul, for example, wrote about "we who are alive, and remain until the coming of the Lord" (1 Thess. 4:15).

The experience of the Early Church as chronicled in the New Testament shows that when every person in the Church believes that Jesus is coming back in his or her lifetime, we can expect to see two powerful effects on the lifestyles of Christians: an extraordinary commitment to *holiness* and radical *generosity* reflected in a phenomenal release of resources for the spreading of the gospel.

Personal Holiness
Personal holiness always increases when people are expecting the Lord's return. The apostle John wrote, "We know that, when He

appears, we shall be like Him, because we shall see Him just like He is. And everyone who has this hope fixed on Him purifies himself, just as He is pure" (1 John. 3:2,3).

When I first became a Christian, my pastor preached basically two messages: "Be saved" and "Jesus is coming back soon!" My sister and I were so convinced that He was going to come back at any time that we would be sad most mornings because He had not come the night before.

One evening, I returned home late to find that neither my parents nor my sister were in the house, and there was no note telling me where they had gone. Then I saw my sister's clothes in a pile on the floor, and I panicked. I thought, *The Lord came and I was left behind!*

WHEN I SAW MY SISTER'S CLOTHES IN A PILE ON THE FLOOR, I PANICKED. I THOUGHT, *THE LORD CAME AND I WAS LEFT BEHIND!*

In sheer horror I pedaled my bike all the way to the pastor's house. I arrived there past midnight and banged on the door so loudly that it probably woke up several neighbors. I still remember my overwhelming relief when the pastor, who was surprised, to say the least, opened the door and saw my agitation. I embraced him, saying, "I was not left behind, I was not left behind. Praise God!" It took a few minutes for me to regain my composure and explain. Reassured, I returned home to learn that my folks had gone to help a family who had suffered a sudden death in their midst.

Expectation of Christ's imminent return profoundly affected the priorities of my childhood church: We served the Lord every day rather than occasionally; we gave generously to missions and evangelism; we did not invest time, effort or finances into anything that could have outlived us but put everything we had into preaching the gospel; and we joyfully transferred to heaven as much as possible, hoping to hasten His coming. However, the most powerful evidence of our belief was our commitment to personal holiness. I vividly remember how time and again I overcame temptation by simply reminding myself that the next few minutes could be the moment when Jesus returned.

Phenomenal Release of Resources

If the imminent return of Christ drives our actions, we will joyfully invest our resources for the sake of hastening His return. Believers in the Early Church had no qualms about selling their properties and laying the proceeds at the feet of the apostles because they believed Jesus would return as soon as the ends of the earth had been reached (see Matt. 24:14). Besides, of what use would property be once the Lord had come? We look further at this extraordinary flow of resources into the Kingdom in the next section.

I believe that the return of this paradigm to the Church—that is, drawing motivation from the Lord's coming soon—will be ushered in by angels. I say this because angels introduced this paradigm to the Early Church. The disciples were gazing into heaven, awestruck after the Lord's ascension, when angels interrupted their reverie to say, in essence, "Why are you just standing there? There is work to be done. Jesus is coming back, so you had better be ready" (see Acts 1:11). So the disciples returned to Jerusalem, where they soon witnessed the first crop of a plentiful harvest. I predict that very soon, angels will begin to show up all over the world to announce that Jesus is coming back soon, creating a powerful accelerator for the end-time harvest.

Paradigm #16:
No Division Between Clergy and Laity

But Peter raised him up, saying, "Stand up; I too am just a man" (Acts 10:26).

The Early Church was led by "uneducated and untrained men" whose only (but most effective) credential was "that they had been with Jesus" (Acts 4:13, *NKJV*). Uneducated does not mean illiterate. The apostles knew how to read and write, and some of them even had business experience, but they had no formal education in religious matters.

This informal form of Church leadership continued during the first few centuries and coincided with an era of rapid expansion of Christianity. Eventually, a division of the Church into clergy and laity was created—a division that severely damaged the effectiveness of the Church by confining to a few, by virtue of their training, the mission that belongs to everyone, by reason of their calling. The wall that was thrown up between these two groups inside the Church—with clergy being superior in rank—is unbiblical. The division is also a corruption of the Early Church model, established as it was with the help of secular rulers, who wanted to use the Church for political purposes.

There is no question that the Lord has provided for governmental offices in the Church for the equipping of the saints for the work of the ministry (see Eph. 4:7-16). The existence of these offices and the need to fill them are undeniable. But there is no basis for the mistaken belief that only members of the so-called clergy should occupy these offices.

The Church is not egalitarian when it comes to government; the existence of these offices attests to that. Nevertheless, divinely ordained levels of leadership should never preclude the

Church from vigorously exercising the priesthood entrusted to all believers. Neither should we confine our priesthood as ministry solely to the Lord. Instead, our efforts must also be directed toward the lost. Doing so will result in our cities being filled with the teaching of the apostles by everyday Christians who minister to everybody, everywhere, on a daily basis. This becomes an absolute necessity when seen in the context of a plentiful harvest!

The need to fill the city with the gospel makes the elimination of this division imperative because it puts an unbearable share of the ministry on a few. For cities to be reached, *this has to change*. Otherwise, the Church will continue to resemble a World Cup final, where 22 exhausted soccer players in desperate need of rest are being watched by thousands of overweight spectators desperately in need of some exercise. Moreover, in the case of the Church, the opposing team does not have just 22 players but hundreds of thousands! There is no way our "pros" can win this match by themselves—every player in the Church must be active and on the field!

The Church Was Not Part of the Establishment

Jesus never envisioned His Church to be run by a religious elite. On the contrary, His design was intentionally nonreligious. Let us review the record:

None of the 12 apostles belonged to the religious establishment. In fact, they were Galileans, a group largely despised by the religious clique in Jerusalem.

None of the leaders in the Early Church were priests or leaders in the Temple. Paul had been a prominent rabbi but was dismissed by the establishment the moment he became a believer in Jesus. In fact, the Early Church looked to marketplace leaders, as opposed to religious leaders. Where would we find these people today?

Peter, John and James—food industry (fishing)
Matthew—IRS/savings and loan manager (tax collector)
Paul—RV manufacturing (tent-making)
Luke—medical doctor
The Seven (see Acts 6)—businessmen
The Ethiopian first convert—banker
Dorcas—manufacturer of *inner* garments
Lydia upscale clothing material distributor
Cornelius—senior military officer
Simon the tanner—leather goods

The Gospels were written by religious outsiders: a medical doctor, a retired tax officer, a fisherman and Mark, who may have been the scion of a wealthy family, the modern equivalent of being the CEO of a private foundation.

The Church wasn't conceived in a religious setting, such as the Temple or a synagogue, but in a private home—most likely owned by a businessman. The Church was then born in a secular setting, the marketplace, as shown under paradigm 5.

When the moment came to introduce a revolutionary principle—that Gentiles could and should be accepted into the Church—God used three marketplace leaders: Peter, Simon and Cornelius (see Acts 10).

Finally, the Church's international headquarters was established in Antioch, most likely to protect it from the religiosity coming out of Jerusalem.

All of these points lead us to conclude that Jesus never intended for the Church to be a subculture but, rather, the *counterculture*. The Church was not meant to assimilate itself into society but to change society by transforming its cities.

The Marketplace Is the Battleground for the City

A group that wishes to take a city or a nation through nonviolent means will target the regional or national markets, because market control results in *de facto* control over the economy, and whoever controls the economy holds the greatest influence over the people. Look at how empires used to rule conquered or colonized nations through the control of trade. There may have been an initial exchange of gunpowder but, ultimately, it was the lopsided, ongoing exchange of wealth that enabled an empire to exercise control over its colonies.

THE HEART OF THE CITY IS THE MARKETPLACE. THIS IS WHERE THE ACTION NEEDS TO BE IF WE ARE TO REACH OUR CITIES.

Likewise, taking the marketplace is essential for taking the city. The heart of the city is not the Church, much less the church building. The Church is the light of the city, but its heart is the marketplace. Cities are often known by a signature skyline made up of buildings that represent the leading corporations in town. This is where the action needs to be if we are to reach our cities.

The first European convert was a businesswoman who dealt in expensive apparel (see Acts 16:14,15). This was immediately followed by a power encounter in the marketplace involving a slave girl with a spirit of divination (see Acts 16:16-21). Luke recounts 22 power encounters in the book of Acts—all of them but one happened in nonreligious settings, most of them in the marketplace. These events had a profound effect on the cities and, in some cases, the outlying regions.

For a city to be transformed, the marketplace must be transformed. The marketplace is where the battle for our cities should be fought, and there is an army already in place that needs to be commissioned and empowered: the so-called laity. Whether they run corporations or work for them, they are better positioned (than the clergy) to transform the marketplace.

Christians in the marketplace already have an anointing to share the gospel with the lost; but, in most cases, the anointing has not been activated, as the laypersons have been relegated to second-class status in the Church.

The Heart of the Marketplace Is the Food Supply

If the marketplace is the heart of the city, what is the marketplace's most vital part? The food supply. Almost anything can go wrong in the market—inflation, political corruption, even a natural disaster—and the city will put up with it and eventually recover. But if the food supply becomes critically insufficient, revolutions happen, rulers lose their heads and chaos ensues—until order is restored, first in the food supply and eventually in all other areas of the marketplace. A calamitous disruption in the food supply is the societal equivalent of a heart attack.

I want to show now how the Early Church brought reconciliation to the marketplace by taking care of the needy. This was their premier strategy for winning multitudes to Christ. They did it by bridging the gap between masters and slaves, the have and the have-nots (see paradigm 4). I believe this strategy was necessary because the marketplace—specifically, the food supply (daily bread, as our Lord called it) or lack thereof—is the arena where spiritual oppression is most painfully felt.

The spiritual oppression generated by the devil is neither abstract nor intangible. Quite the opposite: It is real and it manifests itself as poverty and hunger. In 2 Chronicles 7:14, we are promised that if we get right with God, in addition to forgiving our sins, He will heal the land. This is a clear reference to prosperity. All through the Old Testament we see examples where the penalty for sin, especially idolatry, took the form of famine, pestilence or drought. The rough edge of such a judgment was always felt first in the marketplace and then in the stomachs of the people. It is no coincidence that the poorest nations are those where Christ and His message are known the least. The greater the spiritual oppression, the more rampant are poverty and hunger. This is why we need to bring the message of reconciliation to the marketplace if we are going to reach our cities.

I was steered in this direction by something unusual that happened in the summer of 1999 in La Plata, Argentina, where we went to facilitate a city-reaching plan. Shortly after we arrived in town, the Lord indicated that before we did anything we should go to the main plaza and take a public offering for the Children's Hospital, which was in need of repairs. Taking an offering to help children is not new. What made it unusual was the Lord's two qualifiers: The offering had to be taken publicly, and it had to be done before we did anything else.

We went to the main plaza with a group of 331 overseas delegates and a handful of Argentines. We asked a group of five pastors to stand on a small platform with offering bags in their hands, and we began to put money in them publicly. A total of $8,000 was needed for the repairs, and $11,507 was collected. But that was not the main blessing. While we were taking a public offering, 23 bystanders asked to be led to Christ! I have never seen anything like it! There was no proclamation, no passing out of gospel tracts, nothing. All we did was take a public offering for the neediest people in town—sick children— and 23 persons turned from darkness to light.

Caring for Those in Need Leads to Church Growth

I asked the Lord to show me why this unprecedented thing happened in La Plata. He said to me, "It is not unprecedented. It happened before, and it should happen more often." I then read Acts 2:41-47, the passage where the disciples took care of those who had needs *and the Lord added daily to the Church!*

As I further searched the book of Acts, I found six examples where taking care of the needy, especially the hungry, was followed immediately by growth in the Church:

Care for the Needy	Church Growth
Acts 2:44,45	Acts 2:47
Acts 4:32-35	Acts 5:14,16
Acts 6:1-3	Acts 6:7,8
Acts 10:2,22	Acts: 10:44-48
Acts 11:29	Acts 12:20-24

Marketplace reconciliation was established as a lifestyle (Acts 2:44-47). This is a very straightforward account of how the new believers shared their possessions with the needy. Taking care of the less fortunate was part of the lifestyle of early believers, thereby splicing marketplace reconciliation into the DNA of the Church from the very beginning.

Marketplace reconciliation was threatened by evil from within (Acts 4:32—5:16). Here is a another example of the cause-and-effect relationship between sharing with the needy and the adding of new converts. In this passage, a contrast is presented between Barnabas, who gave well (see Acts 4:36,37), and Ananias and Sapphira, who got it all wrong (see Acts 5:1-10).

Looking at these passages as part of a major thrust helped me to understand why God was so severe with Ananias and Sapphira. If every person who has ever lied (or kept something they had promised God) were to drop dead, I would not be writing this book and you would not be reading it. We would be dead, too. The judgment was so harsh in this case because husband and wife were about to defile the generous flow of merciful acts that produced reconciliation in the marketplace.

They tried to introduce a concept that today is respected, but that in the revival atmosphere of the Early Church was absolutely unacceptable. This popular sentiment goes something like this: *My wealth is my own. If there are social iniquities around, it is not my problem. I bear no responsibility for the needs of others.* Contrast this self-serving belief with Acts 4:32-35:

> And the congregation of those who believed were of one heart and soul; and not one of them claimed that anything belonging to him was his own; but all things were common property to them. . . . And abundant grace was upon them all. For there was not a needy person among them, for all who were owners of land or houses would sell them and bring the proceeds of the sales, and lay them at the apostles' feet; and they would be distributed to each, as any had need.

This is the context against which Ananias and Sapphira's demise took place. And once these two were removed, "multitudes of men and women, were constantly added to" the Church (Acts 5:14).

Taking care of the needy is no small thing as far as God is concerned, and interfering with such efforts is a serious offense.

Marketplace reconciliation was threatened by inadequacy (Acts 6:1-7). In this passage growth was being threatened by a budding grievance: "A complaint arose on the part of the Hellenistic Jews . . . because their widows were being overlooked in the daily serving of food" (Acts 6:1). So the Twelve called the people together and asked that seven men be chosen to deal with what was apparently a supply-and-demand problem related to food distribution.

Traditionally, it has been assumed that the chosen ones became the first deacons and that they served tables. Neither belief is sustained by the passage. The word "deacon" does not appear anywhere in the chapter, and we know the men were not chosen to serve the tables personally for three reasons: (1) as soon as the apostles laid hands on them, two went into dynamic, all-consuming ministries; (2) there is no report that they served tables; and (3) it would have been physically impossible for just seven men to serve tables for a group that numbered in the thousands.

These seven were likely chosen for their business experience, and as soon as they were anointed for the task, "the word of God kept on spreading; and the number of the disciples continued to increase greatly in Jerusalem" (Acts 6:7). I believe the mention of Jerusalem right after the seven were chosen is a reference to the fact that the complaint described in verse 1 had threatened to spread there. Thanks to the chosen seven, the issue ceased to be a problem.

Marketplace leaders opened the Church to Gentiles (Acts 10:2,22,44-48). The events of Acts 10 precipitated what was then the greatest paradigm shift in the emerging Church. The apostle Peter, a businessman, was staying in the home of another businessman, Simon, the tanner, when he received a vision from the Lord. The next day God used that vision to convince Peter to meet with Cornelius, a Gentile and a senior officer in the Roman army that controlled Judea. In effect, Romans were the masters and the Jews their slaves. Nevertheless, God chose a leader like Cornelius to bridge that gap because he exhibited two powerful traits needed for reconciliation: First, he gave alms to the poor among the Jews, an extremely unusual gesture for a Roman; second, he knelt before Peter, a sign of great humility. Cornelius's messengers referred to his good reputation among the Jews and to his godly character to convince Peter that he should go with them (see v. 22).

Peter went and after he shared the gospel, Cornelius's entire household and close friends came to the Lord and received the Holy Spirit (see vv. 44-48). This most extraordinary event, particularly the outpouring of the Spirit upon the household, led the other apostles to see that Gentiles were welcome in the Church as well (see Acts 11:18). To proclaim this momentous revelation God used three marketplace leaders, one of whom was well known all over the nation for his compassion for the poor.

Marketplace injustice was judged (Acts 11:27-30; 12:20-25). The newly established Church in Antioch was warned by a prophet of a coming famine in Judea. They immediately took an offering and sent it with Barnabas and Saul to the brethren in Judea.

In the meantime, the Church in Jerusalem and Judea was in the midst of a severe trial. Peter and James had been arrested. The former was set free by an angel, while the latter was put to death by the sword. The evil genius behind this persecution was Herod, who was also angry with the people of Tyre and Sidon. They had sent a delegation asking for peace because their country was fed by Herod's country. The situation must have been critical because by now the famine was in full swing. If Herod was angry at Tyre and Sidon, it is safe to assume that he must have been withholding food.

One day, Herod gave an address, apparently with so much pride that an angel of the Lord struck him dead. We see here the same dynamics that operated in the case of Ananias and Sapphira. Apparently Herod thought of himself as a god who exercised final authority over what to do with food in a time of famine, and God judged him severely. Even though it is not explicitly stated, because of the context it seems likely that Herod was killed because he was withholding food from people in a time of famine. After he was removed, the gospel continued to spread and Barnabas and Saul completed their mission (see Acts 12:24,25). What was their mission? To bring relief to those affected by the famine. The correlation between helping the needy and the growth of the Church is hard to miss.

The Defining Mark of an Apostle

We see in these passages a direct correlation between caring for the needy and large numbers of people coming to the Lord. Caring for those in need is the tangible expression of the intangible reconciliation between the haves and the have-nots. This issue was so central to the attitudes and practices of the Early Church that when Paul went to Jerusalem to defend his apostleship, Peter, James and John gave him only one admonition: "Remember the poor" (Gal. 2:10)—something that Paul was eager to do. It is fascinating that this was their only recommendation, sort of a litmus test: If you are an apostle, you must take care of the poor. Many so-called apostles fail this test today.

This is consistent with what Paul said in his farewell speech to the Church in Ephesus:

> You yourselves know that these hands ministered to my own needs and to the men who were with me. In everything I showed you that by working hard in this manner you must help the weak and remember the words of the Lord Jesus, that He Himself said, "It is more blessed to give than to receive" (Acts 20:34,35).

Paul made two important points here: First, that we must take care of the weak (needy), according to his apostolic example; second, it is all right to work hard at one's secular profession while "teaching . . . publicly and from house to house" (Acts 20:20). Paul must have worked very hard as a tentmaker to provide for himself, his team and the weak they encountered. This is a lot of people, and I am sure it took a lot of tents!

The Need for Power Encounters

Power encounters merit a mention here. The leaders in the Early Church were marketplace leaders who combined their previous marketplace expertise with their newfound spiritual power to effect reconciliation between those who had a lot and those who had little or nothing. They did this not only through extreme generosity but also through power encounters.

The traditional bent among Christian business people has been toward the use of charity to alleviate iniquities and inequalities in the marketplace, but seldom have signs and wonders been employed to change the spiritual cause and resulting conditions that create these problems in the marketplace.

The Church has worked signs and wonders to change individual lives, but rarely institutions. This is why we believe in Christian businesspeople but we still do not believe in Christian businesses. The axiom is that Christians can survive in business, but they can never change the ungodly structures and market environment that give them so much trouble. Quite often the business practices we encounter are so evil and anti-God that we feel helpless to do anything to effect change in the marketplace. This is where signs and wonders can be helpful.

As mentioned earlier, the book of Acts records numerous examples of power encounters in the marketplace that resulted in tangible change. There are several reasons for this. One is that the marketplace is the heart of the city and the Early Church was focused on reaching the city. Another is that the marketplace exhibited tangible proof of evil, institutional evil, as evidenced by the exploitation of the weak and needy.

THE MARKETPLACE IS A CITADEL OF THE ENEMY, BUT IT CAN BE TAKEN BY DISPLACING SATAN'S CONTROL THROUGH SIGNS AND WONDERS.

A third reason is that supernatural evil, often expressed through idolatry, was firmly entrenched in the marketplace and used its position to exercise spiritual control over entire cities and regions, as in the case of Ephesus (see Acts 19:11-27). This is why it is crucial that the Church today see the marketplace as a citadel of the enemy that needs to be taken by displacing his control through signs and wonders.

My friend and associate Rick Heeren is breaking new ground in this area. He has developed a biblical method for introducing signs and wonders into the marketplace. His upcoming book, tentatively titled *Marketplace Christian*, captures the essence of this much-needed emphasis.

Market Leaders Made Excellent Church Leaders

Paul appointed elders shortly after planting a city Church, and he picked them from among relatively new converts. It is remarkable that these elders did so well, even those appointed in cities where there was fierce persecution. Most likely Paul chose them from among those who already held positions of leadership in the marketplace. As the last and greatest revival draws near, we need to commission the 99 percent of the Church that already lives and works in the marketplace to operate there in the power of the Holy Spirit. When every "lay" person is able to see his or her place of work the way pastors see their congregations, then flowing in the power of the Holy Spirit, they will be able to turn their offices and workstations into beachheads. Furthermore, their seasoned and proven leadership will take city-reaching thrusts to higher levels.

Rich Marshall's book *God @ Work* (Destiny Image) is a challenging treatise on the need to tear down this wall that has long hindered the mission of the Church. We believe so strongly in the need to expedite the onset of this new paradigm that everywhere we go to facilitate city reaching, Marshall and Heeren are an integral part of the effort.

I find it spiritually invigorating to watch men and women receive God's anointing to take the kingdom of God to their workplaces. Let us keep moving in that direction until His kingdom comes to the city in force!

Paradigm #17:
The Spirit of the Lord Poured Upon All Flesh

"AND IT SHALL BE IN THE LAST DAYS," God says, "THAT I WILL POUR FORTH OF MY SPIRIT UPON ALL MANKIND; AND YOUR SONS AND YOUR DAUGHTERS SHALL PROPHESY, AND YOUR YOUNG MEN SHALL SEE VISIONS, AND YOUR OLD MEN SHALL DREAM DREAMS; EVEN UPON MY BONDSLAVES, BOTH MEN AND WOMEN, I WILL IN THOSE DAYS POUR FORTH OF MY SPIRIT and they shall proph-

esy. AND I WILL GRANT WONDERS IN THE SKY ABOVE,
AND SIGNS ON THE EARTH BENEATH, BLOOD, AND FIRE,
AND VAPOR OF SMOKE. THE SUN SHALL BE TURNED
INTO DARKNESS, AND THE MOON INTO BLOOD, BEFORE
THE GREAT AND GLORIOUS DAY OF THE LORD SHALL
COME. AND IT SHALL BE THAT EVERYONE WHO CALLS
ON THE NAME OF THE LORD SHALL BE SAVED" (Acts
2:17-21).

This paradigm represents the fulfillment of Joel's prophecy as
quoted by Peter during the first message of the Church age. This
passage announces the pouring out of God's Spirit upon all
flesh, that is, upon the entire world population. This means that
the Spirit of God will be poured out upon everybody in your city.
Awesome!

The focus of this universal outpouring is evangelistic, as it
climaxes with the statement that "EVERYONE WHO CALLS ON
THE NAME OF THE LORD SHALL BE SAVED" (Acts 2:21). One cannot get more evangelistic than that—God's Spirit touches everybody and everyone who calls on Him gets saved and joins a community of transformed people.

Jim Munson shared with me two contrasting pictures of the
Church, and I want to share them with you. First, let us look at
the biblical example:

All the believers were together and had everything in common. They sold their possessions and goods and gave to anyone
who had need. Every day they met in the Temple courts. They
broke bread in their homes and ate together with glad and sin-
cere hearts, praising God and enjoying the favor of all the people. And the Lord added to their number daily all those who
were being saved (see Acts 2:44-47).

Now let us consider the opposite of the biblical model:

All the believers kept to themselves and had few common interests. They held tight to their possessions and goods, and they tried to avoid anyone in need who might take advantage of them or take what was rightfully theirs. They met together at church on Sunday and on special occasions. They ate at home with ritualized prayer and false cheer, smiling on the outside but full of grumbling and discontentment on the inside, forgetting to praise or thank God and lacking in favor or respect from other people. *And the Lord had no reason at all to send others to them.*

These are the two options before us. Praise God, He has promised to pour out His Spirit upon all flesh for multitudes to be transformed in these last days, first in the Church and then in the city.

Joel's prophecy also predicts full reconciliation among all peoples. Old and young, male and female, free and slave, male and female—all are shown ministering in unity and working in harmony. This, in turn, makes possible the fullness of the Spirit in the Church, so that the Spirit of the Lord will spill out and touch all flesh. When this happens, the kingdom of God will be in evidence all over the world. Then Jesus' return should be just a moment away!

9

WHERE DO WE GO FROM HERE?

*In a journey of a thousand miles
the most important step is the first.
Nothing else can happen
until that first step is taken.*

Moses looked out over the Red Sea, surrounded by hundreds of thousands of frightened former slaves. Pharaoh's murderous army was visible in the distance behind them, and they were rapidly closing. Moses had to make a decision. Going back was suicidal, but going forward looked impossible. Nevertheless, forward was the only way to go.

As he gazed at the Red Sea, Moses knew he could look at the opposite shore and be overwhelmed by the distance, or he could find a place to put his foot down on the shore closest to him. He chose the latter and the sea parted, and in no time, Moses and his people were safely on the other shore while Pharaoh's army drowned.

In a journey of a thousand miles the most important step is the first one. Nothing else happens until that first step is taken. If you are a pastor, how do you move a stalled city-reaching thrust forward? Or how do you get one up and moving if there is nothing yet in place? The general road map is provided in *That None Should Perish*, where I suggested these six steps, to be performed in order:

1. *Establish God's perimeter* by meeting regularly with other leaders who have the same vision and passion. Begin to pray together.
2. *Secure God's perimeter* by dealing within the microcosm of this gathering with every problem affecting the Church and the city—racism, bigotry, selfishness, anger, etc. Go heavy on prophetic acts to expose the lies of the evil one and to destroy the veneer of immutability with which he has coated those lies.
3. *Expand God's perimeter* by reaching out to others whom God touched while you were doing steps 1 and 2. This includes intercessors, youth and marketplace leaders in addition to other pastors.
4. *Invade Satan's perimeter* by launching lighthouses of prayer. This will spread all over what you and the other leaders have developed in one part of the city. I suggest that this be done in a coordinated, sweeping effort. The objective must be to pray for everybody in town on a regular basis.
5. *Attack and destroy Satan's perimeter* by using the one-week exercise described in this book.

6. *Establish God's perimeter where Satan's used to be* by identi-
    fying the ugliest mark of the devil on the Church and
    erasing it through a prophetic act that embodies the
    opposite trait or implication.

In Resistencia, where Satan's mark was clearly mistrust and
division, the pastors chose to hold a united baptismal service for
new converts. The service was held in a covered arena where the
pastors had arranged portable swimming pools to form the
shape of a cross. The old-timers sat on bleachers, while the new
converts stood by the pools, alongside the pastors of the city.
After an initial prayer declaring their allegiance to Jesus Christ,
the new believers got into the pools and were baptized into the
only Church in the city: the Church of Jesus Christ!

These steps work and have proven valid. However, we have
learned much more about this process since the first book—
especially about how to jump-start a city-reaching thrust that
has stalled.

Competency Versus Commitment

A person who scores very high in *competency* usually scores very
low on *commitment* when it comes to participating in something new that falls outside his or her immediate area of concern or giftedness. Generally speaking, pastors and congregations who have the greatest resources and the most talented
people seem to be the ones who are less willing to make a substantive commitment to city reaching, unless the thrust is or
becomes an outgrowth of what *they* are already doing. The reason is that they have a program to run and cannot be distract-
ed for long.

This attitude is not new. We see it when pastors feel they *have* to do something together that is not a part of their own pro-

DAVID'S ARMY WAS

NOT MADE UP OF

WEST POINT GRADUATES.

THEY WERE MOSTLY

SOCIAL MISFITS,

BUT THEY WERE

TOTALLY COMMITTED.

grams—for instance, a citywide crusade with a prestigious evangelist. When the pastors show up for the planning meeting, the usually unspoken question is the same: *What is the minimum investment we need to make for the shortest amount of time to get the maximum return?* One reason for this is that the event in question is not central to the programs in which their congregations are actively engaged.

To deal effectively with the tension between competency and commitment, you need to know that God has called *you* to do something for the Church and for the city and that you should *do it*, regardless of whether you stand to reap any personal or ministerial benefits. This requires an extraordinary change in thinking, as it goes against everything we have been trained to do and have done in the past.

If you have been chosen for the task, do everything God tells you to do, regardless of how you figure to rate on the competency scale. You won't be the only one who is starting at a low competency level. David's army was not made up of West Point graduates. They were mostly social misfits; but because *they were totally committed* to David, they took him to the throne of Israel.

The main point is this: Leaders, go for those who exhibit commitment, because commitment is a voluntary attitude that cannot be imposed, whereas competency is a set of skills that can be taught.

Cohesiveness Versus Inclusiveness

When a city-reaching thrust is first launched, the tendency is to include as many people as possible instead of beginning with those few who have a high degree of cohesiveness regarding purpose and strategy. There is a natural tension between cohesiveness and inclusiveness.

Cohesion is the quality that produces "the molecular attraction by which the particles of a body are united."[1] A less sophisticated definition of cohesiveness would be "the ability to stick together." Inclusiveness is the intent "to take in or comprise as a part of a whole."[2]

The tendency toward inclusiveness and the need for cohesiveness create a tension that has to be resolved, and there is no magic formula. However, it is clearly a mistake to include as many pastors as possible too soon. If you bring every pastor in town on board right away, you will have 100 percent inclusiveness but close to 0 percent cohesiveness because most of them are bound to have different agendas.

The wisest course of action, in the early stages, is to resist the impulse toward inclusiveness. Lean toward cohesiveness without becoming exclusionist. This needs to be done until God's perimeter is firmly established and secured. Then you can move toward inclusiveness by expanding God's perimeter (see step 3). To do this successfully, however, you need to be aware of four things:

- *God does not abide by majority votes.* God does not require a majority to be on His side in order to move. In fact, time and again God settled for one person *if* that person submitted to Him and was willing to serve others. The Bible provides many examples of God changing the lives of many through one person—Abraham, Joseph, Moses, etc. In Revelation, Jesus says seven times, "He who has an ear, let him hear what the Spirit says to the churches."[3] One person is enough for God, even if that person is listening with only half his natural capability.

- *Strongholds are very vulnerable.* The spiritual strongholds over your city are far more vulnerable than they appear to be. They are like the Goodyear blimp hovering over stadiums during televised football games; it looks impressive and indestructible, but how many holes would it take to bring it down? Only one. Likewise, the Grand Coulee Dam, with its trillions of tons of reinforced concrete, looks impregnable; but one tiny crack would render it useless *immediately*.

- *Prophetic acts are very powerful.* The group of pastors who implement steps 1 and 2 can shatter every stronghold over the city through prophetic acts performed inside the newly established beachhead. Please notice, I said *shatter* and not *bring down*. That will happen later in step 3. This is where prophetic acts will play a decisive role.

- *Ministerial associations have limitations.* Generally speaking, the ministerial association is not the best vehicle for a city-reaching thrust. Such associations have to maintain a broad base of interest and related activities that make it very difficult for cohesiveness to develop around a single focus, as required for city reaching. However, ministerial associations should not been shunned, much less undermined, since they play an important role in the city now and *even more so* in the future. Your group needs to be part of it; but at the same time, you need a more cohesive forum to develop a prototype for city reaching.

This is what I suggest you do to resolve the tension between cohesiveness and inclusiveness:

Ask permission to establish a city reaching/prayer evangelism department *within* the ministerial association. Assure the ministerial leadership that you will continue to support the regular activities of the association. It is very important that you have their spiritual covering, or at least their blessing.

Define the objectives, goals and strategy for the new department strictly along the lines of prayer evangelism. Everyone should be invited to participate, but only those who subscribe to the objectives should join. In other words, set up a narrow gate and build a large corral behind it. Use the narrowness of the gate to attract primarily people who display a high degree of cohesiveness and commitment.

Make it part of the strategy for the city-reaching team to pray together *weekly*. A commitment to being *together* in addition to being in *one accord* should be a defining characteristic of those who join in. Praying together weekly has at least three positive effects: First, watchmen on the wall will help to improve the spiritual climate; second, it provides a source of prayer support for all the activities of the ministerial association, making them more successful; third, it establishes you and your team as the builders of the prayer shield over the city, something that will prove highly strategic when you decide to expand the perimeter (step 3).

Seven Steps to Maximize Cohesiveness

Once the foundational work described above is completed, I suggest a seven-step process to produce enough cohesiveness to mobilize the Church in the city.

To understand how such a small part can pull the whole, I suggest you try this simple exercise in physics: Take 10 toothpicks and break 9 of them into smaller pieces, leaving the tenth one intact. Next, throw them randomly into a basin filled with water. After a while, check on them. You will see the smaller pieces bunched around the bigger one, either directly or indirectly. How did this happen? The greater mass of the big piece provided the pull necessary to bring in the smaller ones. This is what the exercise I am about to suggest is designed to accomplish. To have enough mass to pull the other parts, you don't have to be bigger than the whole; you only have to be bigger than each individual part.

The seven steps suggested below are very simple. Do not allow their simplicity to cause you to underestimate their potential for establishing a vortex of cohesiveness in your city. These steps should be done by everybody in the group of leaders who pray together. The group's members should be accountable to each other, and they should review individual progress weekly to ensure that *everybody* is moving along simultaneously.

Step 1: Begin to pray for your neighbors. Make them your flock. Apply the four steps listed in Luke 10 and discussed at length in chapter 2. Once you are doing it, you will talk about it in sermons, counseling, Sunday school class and personal conversations. Prayer evangelism will become part of your philosophy of ministry, and your people will eventually emulate your example.

Step 2: Ask your family to join you. Share the principles of prayer evangelism with your spouse and children. Make it interesting and exciting. Write down the names of the people you are praying for as a family. Put them in a container and during meals have everyone pick a name, pray for that person and move them to a second container until you have prayed for everyone. Repeat the procedure daily.

Step 3: Enlist your paid staff to do it. By paid staff I mean anyone who is on the payroll: associates, receptionist, janitor, etc. You certainly can define their jobs because they are *your* staff. Share the principles with them and ask them to take up the task as part of their jobs. Meet with them weekly to monitor their progress.

Step 4: Challenge your paid staff to have their families join in. Meet with them as a group and bring your family along to share how they are doing it.

Step 5: Invite your unpaid staff to do it. This group is the one that usually is in your corner, no matter what. This group includes ushers, Sunday School teachers, parking attendants, etc. They are the ones who serve without pay because they like you. It should be easy to sign them up.

Step 6: Enlist the families of your unpaid staff the same way you did in step 4. At this point in time, you should have everybody who is in leadership in your congregation as well as their immediate families involved in modeling prayer evangelism. This is bound to have an impact on the rest of your congregation.

Step 7: All the pastors in your group should bring their congregations together for a time of testimony and celebration. Track every lighthouse of prayer on a wall map for the audience to see. Also, make copies of the map for individuals. Highlight the most dramatic testimonies, and also make room for the simpler ones. Emphasize the number of lost people who are being prayed for regularly in the city. Then enlist new recruits.

When you reach step 7, you should have achieved optimum cohesiveness in your group. Now is the time to move toward inclusiveness by reaching out to the rest of the pastors and leaders in your city with a prototype that is both tangible and easy to duplicate. Going back to the physics example, your group should have enough mass to begin to pull the Church in the city.

Beverly Jaime, of Cathedral of Faith in San Jose, California, has developed the best training kit for helping to move the process along the seven steps listed here.[4]

At Harvest Evangelism, we have developed a couple of accelerators that can help you to expedite this process. One way to accelerate your program is by sending a team to Argentina to participate in one of our summer or fall training programs, where we teach how to reach a city by *actually reaching a city*. This has proven so effective that in all the cities where we are currently working, there is at least one person in leadership who has participated in one of these programs.[5]

Another way you can accelerate the process is to attend one of our City Reachers Schools. Or you may want to explore the possibility of having us hold one in your city. These schools incorporate the three-day radio launch of lighthouses of prayer mentioned in this book. The best time to host a City Reachers School is right after step 7, when the school can expand your perimeter by making the rest of the Church in your city aware of what is going on in your group.

Resolving Tensions

As the city-reaching thrust begins to move toward inclusiveness, the success of the effort will depend largely on resolving natural tensions on several fronts. Understand that these tensions should not be eliminated but, rather, you should use them to move the thrust forward, as with the tension between the sail and the rudder on a sailboat. By positioning the sail and the rudder at the right angle, the pilot transforms tension into thrust that propels the boat through contrary winds.

5-15-80 Formula

C. Peter Wagner made the observation that only 5 percent of the people in the Church are visionaries, that is, individuals who can actually *see the invisible*. Another 15 percent are implementers who can carry out the vision with a minimum of assistance. The other 80 percent need a program to guide them step by step through the process. When they hear a vision described in the abstract, they are not interested because they cannot see it. On the other hand, when the vision is translated into a plan or a program, they can easily implement it.

Because program-driven people compose a majority, it is important to be aware that sooner or later the tendency will be to move them into leadership. If this is done too hastily or in a way that displaces the visionaries from the helm, the *process* will degenerate into a *program* and will soon die. The key to resolving this tension is to always keep the visionaries on the bridge and the implementers in the boiler room. Both have been equipped by God in a unique way. Connecting them and keeping them in their places of greatest effectiveness is key to the ultimate success of the city-reaching thrust.

Local Churches Versus Parachurch Ministries

Parachurch ministries generally are more focused on reaching the lost than are local churches. They bring to a citywide effort a sense of urgency and singleness of focus that makes them highly effective in helping to initiate the process. On the other hand, the ability to sustain a city-reaching effort depends entirely on the local churches. Often, there is a history of significant tension, deep hurts and mistrust between the congregations and parachurch ministries in a city.

It helps to understand that neither "local church" nor "parachurch ministry" is a biblical term. What we call a local church is not a church but a local congregation that, along with many others, forms the Church in the city. And parachurch (outside the Church) is a misnomer since no Christian ministry can operate *outside* of *the* Church. I suggest that both monikers be dropped. Parachurch groups could be called "servant ministries," while local churches should be referred to as "local congregations."

Both are valid expressions of the Church. Reconciliation must take place between both camps; they need to sit at the same table as peers as both are equally essential to the city-reaching thrust. Also, both parties need to be in mutual submission and be given latitude to operate within their particular giftings.

Every enterprise needs a man of war and a man of peace. The so-called parachurch ministries fit the profile of the former; the local churches, the latter. Let the servant ministries take the point, raiding the enemy camp as the avant-garde of a marching Church instead of as disconnected guerrilla bands. And let the local congregations move in behind them to settle the new frontier. The sooner this tension is resolved, the sooner the Church will be able to fight a coordinated offensive and defensive war.

Programmatic Unity Versus Organic Unity

There are many worthwhile efforts in a city that build unity around a program, such as crusades, concerts of prayer or door-to-door visitation campaigns. Because the unity they build is centered on a program and is inevitably fleeting, these programs can pose a threat to the deeper type of unity required to operate as one Church in the city. However, they should not be despised or opposed. Participating in them provides an opportunity to make known to others what God is doing in you and through you, and this in turn can lead to greater interest and to the others' eventual participation in the city-reaching thrust. However, caution is required lest those events clutter the agenda to the point of smothering everything else.

Generally speaking, traditional mass evangelistic crusades have the potential to stall city reaching on two counts: (1) when it's over, they leave the false impression that evangelism has been done, and (2) they deplete the Church of human and financial resources to the point that usually it takes a minimum of two years to recover.

If such a crusade becomes inevitable, it is wise to incorporate prayer evangelism and lighthouses of prayer *at the front end* and to do this early in the pre-crusade planning. This will increase the prayer covering for the crusade and will mobilize the Church to reach out to the lost. Both of these are highly desired by evangelists, and they should welcome the suggestion.

Pastoral Roles Versus Apostolic Roles

Pastors are the spiritual gatekeepers of the city, and they need to wear two hats: a pastoral hat, because of the congregations they lead, and an apostolic hat, because of the city-reaching thrust they are involved in. It is essential that pastors know *when* to wear which hat. When pastors involved in city reaching come together, the guiding principle should be what is good for the Church rather than for their individual congregations. Failure to do so will result in a spiritual co-op, where partners invest only to the degree that they can get a personal return.

Ray Stedman, in his classic book *Body Life*, writes about two biblical lists of gifts: Romans 12 and 1 Corinthians 12 describe "*gifts given to people* in the Church," whereas Ephesians 4 talks about "*gifted people* given to the Church." The basic difference is that an Ephesians 4 person, including the apostle, is a gift given not to a specific congregation, but to the Church *as a whole*. When the facilitating group comes together, it must operate as an Ephesians 4 group.

Servanthood Versus Leadership

One of the proven blessings of the city-reaching movement is that it convenes some of the best people in the world. These men and women love the Lord, the Church and the lost. They hate the devil, and they are willing to pay any price to see the kingdom of God come to the city. Above all else, they are genuinely humble people.

However, because they are so humble, they need to be aware that the devil will likely not tempt them with pride, as it is so foreign to them. Instead, the devil will often tempt them with *excessive* humility, which is pride in reverse. Pride overshoots while excessive humility undershoots, but both miss the mark.

Time and again I have seen the faithful remnant succumb to this scheme of the devil. They work hard to set a wonderful table; and when the time comes to call the guests to enjoy what they have prepared, instead of sitting at the head of the table, they look for someone else to do it. Many times the one who takes that place is someone who is *not* humble and the city reaching thrust ends up being hijacked and often derailed.

The best antidote against excessive humility is to recognize that it is pride in disguise. Basically, it is a form of fear of man, which places us in a position to be cursed, for "cursed is the man who trusts in mankind" (Jer. 17:5). The drive for human approval distracts us from the fundamental principle that leaders should aspire not to be liked but to be respected. The ability to make the right decisions, no matter the cost, is what will generate that respect.

Jesus said, "Whoever exalts himself shall be humbled; and whoever humbles himself shall be exalted" (Matt. 23:12). If God has exalted you and placed you in a position of leadership, then you need to do what God has equipped you to do. If the plane I am traveling on is about to land in the midst of a fierce storm, I do not want the captain to come over the loudspeaker to say, "Who am I, a humble servant of God, to land this plane? I am totally unworthy. Would someone else come forward and take my place?" No! I want and I *expect* the captain to land that plane because he is the one who has been entrusted with that responsibility. So do you.

WE BECAME THE BEST CHOICE FOR THE JOB THE DAY GOD CHOSE US. LET US WALK ACCORDING TO HIS CALLING.

None of us would be man's first choice for the job at hand—there is always someone else who is better qualified. However, we became the best choice the day God chose us. We are qualified not because of our personal attributes, but because of God's sovereign calling. Let us walk according to His calling.

Charismatics, Conservatives and Mainliners

When it comes to reaching cities, God will not favor the charismatics or the conservatives or the mainliners. He will use *the* Church, which is made up of many streams. It is fundamental to know *at all times* that it will take the *whole* Church to present the *whole* gospel to the *whole* city. Anything short of that constitutes sectarianism arising from the ignoring or despising of the redemptive gifts entrusted to the other streams. Charismatics bring to the table a unique awareness of the Holy Spirit and His gifts. Conservatives have a deep respect for the written Word of God and for the theological reflection that emanates from it. Mainliners have a deep and practical compassion for the poor, the needy and the downtrodden. None of these can stand alone, but together, they exemplify the fullness of Christ in the Church.

Focus, Alignment and Closure

So where do we go from here? Up and forward! In addition to the steps discussed in this chapter, here are three key components to keep in mind.

Focus

The focus of the city-reaching thrust should always be clear and absolutely non-negotiable: to reach your city through prayer evangelism. Keep it simple and constant. By simple, I mean do not add to it; and by constant, I mean keep doing it and do not stop until you are done! A recurring obstacle is that after a major breakthrough in the city, the leaders are bombarded with offers by powerful, hard-to-ignore ministries that "feel led to come to your city." Some of those ministries have something to contribute, and others don't. If the latter are allowed to come in and compromise the Church's focus, the thrust will slow down and gradually come to a complete stop.

Establish the focus and keep at it until you have reached level 4 (see the definition for a city reached in chapter 5). Do not let *anything* distract you.

Alignment

We have identified five key affinity groups that need to be developed and aligned within the city-reaching thrust: pastors, intercessors, youth, marketplace leaders and ethnic leaders. The pastors are the spiritual gatekeepers; the other four provide tracks into the city. Each of these groups should be developed using the seven-step process suggested earlier in this chapter. And once they have been developed, they need to be aligned for *maximum impact*. During the culminating weeklong thrust, these groups should be used as divisions that are deployed forward to attack simultaneously and destroy Satan's perimeter all over the city.

Closure

You need to finally bring closure to the city-reaching thrust. This sounds obvious, but it is not so obvious once you get going, especially if you meet with some initial success. Time and again we have seen pastors satisfied with looting a few tents when they could have had the whole camp! They should never be satisfied with just *some growth* in their congregations. Closure means seeing the *entire* city reached and a huge harvest piling up at the doors. Anything short of that is less than excellent. By committing to a timetable and stating that by a specific date you will have done this and that, you introduce an irreversible element of closure.

That All Should Hear

Let me challenge you to make a decision to go for your city *now*. You have nothing to fear but fear itself. You are the light of the city because Jesus said that you are the light of the world (see Matt. 5:14). Light always defeats darkness *if taken out from under the bed*. Go for your city today!

What is the worst that can happen? You fail to reach your city? We should die in the attempt rather than vegetate writing or reading books about why it cannot be done. Go for it. Be like those brave men of David, who risked their lives for a glass of water because it was for the king. Do it for the King of kings!

Do not listen to the prophets of doom, those who have compiled a list of reasons why it can't be done. Instead, take your counsel from God and *His* Word. All through this book I have highlighted the Word of God. Let that Word generate faith in you now, and go forward!

Charge ahead. There is a city waiting to hear the voice of God. Whether you are the soldier who conquers the city and plants His flag on the highest point or the one who carries the flag only a short distance forward before being downed by enemy fire, *it does not matter*. God will always be pleased with a soldier who is willing to fight to the finish. Go for it. Millions are waiting to hear the good news.

Notes

1. *Merriam-Webster's Collegiate Dictionary*, 10th ed., s.v. "cohesion."
2. Ibid., s.v. "inclusive."
3. Rev. 2:7,11,17,29; 3:6,13,22.
4. Beverly Jaime, "How to Be a Lighthouse of Prayer." This self-published resource can be obtained on the Internet at www.lighthouseofprayer.org.
5. For more details on our Argentina training programs, visit our website at www.harvestevan.org or call Harvest Evangelism in California at (800) 898-8004.

10

ARE YOU READY?

*To see your city or your nation transformed, you need to move to
a higher level of leadership. You need to go to God's Officer
Candidate School, where the devil is the drill sergeant.*

I am writing this final chapter in the city of Manila in the
Philippines. My team and I are here at the invitation of the
Philippine Prayer Evangelism Network, an organization that is
working with national and local leaders to reach the nation for
Christ through prayer evangelism.

The country is going through a difficult time. Guerilla troops
are holding the government in check in the Mindanao area. The
national economy has plummeted and is close to crashing.
Hunger is fast becoming a reality to many in this beautiful nation.
The president, Joseph Estrada, is under attack from within and
from without. *Time* magazine featured Estrada on the cover of its
Asian edition with the headline, "He Is in Over His Head."

Most Christians in the Philippines did not vote for this president, whose campaign was supported by one of the major cults in this region. There have been questions about his character and integrity, and there is now widespread sentiment among Filipino believers that Estrada was not God's choice to lead the nation. Many of them believe that the nation's woes are, in fact, God's judgment on the Philippines. However, after we taught on the need to pray for those in authority and to speak peace over them, national Christian leaders agreed that it was time to bless the president in a tangible way.

Everyone present was invited to write a blessing on a piece of paper that would then be delivered to President Estrada. The Lord moved among the 2,500 seminar participants, and soon a huge pile of written blessings materialized next to the platform.

Would this make a difference? Would the president even notice?

Less than 24 hours later, a cabinet minister was standing on the platform, accepting the package of blessings. She thanked us and begged us to pray that God would put a stop to the attacks of the demonic forces buffeting the nation. Dan Belays, chairman of the Philippine Prayer Evangelism Network, invited pastors to gather around this representative of the president, and a powerful prayer was said. The envoy was then asked to tell the president that Jesus is knocking at the door of the presidential palace, and that if the president opens the door, He will come in. Deeply moved, she agreed and asked us to pray that when she conveyed our message to the president, he would indeed invite Jesus in.

The next morning, three members of the presidential family came to our hotel seeking prayer, and all these received the Lord. We then showed them how to intercede for the president on a daily basis. The day I left the Philippines, I received an invitation from President Estrada himself to discuss prayer with him at the palace the next time I was in Manila. God got the attention of the president because a relatively small group of Christians chose to obey God's command to pray for those in authority.

These Christians are now determined to see the kingdom of God come to the Philippines. They plan to link every city, town and village via radio to light the nation with lighthouses of prayer. This is serious business.

If you entertain similar hopes and dreams, you need to prepare for the coming of the Kingdom. Allow me to share with you a few final thoughts and important lessons that need to be learned and applied if we are going to see our cities and nations transformed by the power of God.

More Power

My friend Mike Richardson likes to say that his is "the theology of more."[1] By this he means that no matter how much he knows about God, he always wants to know more. This is a very healthy perspective. No matter how much theology we study, there is always more we can know about God. Every day we need more of Him. God gave me a refresher course in theology right here in the Philippines.

In the early morning hours before our seminar was to begin in Manila, something extraordinary happened in my hotel room. I had gone to bed the night before after a rich and fruitful time of prayer with the national Christian leaders. I had heard exciting reports of Filipino pastors being reconciled, neighborhoods being transformed and Muslim tribes in the south being impacted by prayer evangelism. Intercessors had prayer walked the stadium where thousands would gather the next day to study the principles captured in a beautiful syllabus with a full-color cover displaying the legend "Light the Nation Through Prayer Evangelism." Now filled with expectation, I was ready and eager to begin teaching. Before closing my eyes to go to sleep, I had asked God to give me an extra measure of His presence.

At 3:22 A.M. I was awakened by the most beautiful feeling of God's presence. I knew He was in the room. I could feel Him. I fell out of bed and onto my knees, and with anticipation I began to approach His presence in prayer. All of the sudden I was stopped. I had hit something in the spirit. It felt like a clear glass wall; I was on one side and God's presence was on the other. The glass wall was preventing me from entering deeper into His presence.

I asked God why that wall was there, and He impressed upon me a very sobering message: *Ed, you are not thirsty enough to come to the waters to drink. You are full of good things, dreams, ideas and hopes. They are good, but good is not excellent. You are doing the right thing, but you are not doing it the right way. You are not depending on Me!*

Then the Lord took me to chapter 1 in the book of Acts. There He showed me how the disciples had been with Jesus, heard His voice, seen angels and been in prayer, and *still* they had not experienced the fullness of the power of the Holy Spirit. Yet they felt good about themselves, and they decided to do something spiritual: fill the vacancy left by Judas's departure. They read the Scriptures and they prayed, asking God for guidance.

The Lord told me that I was trying to do city reaching the same way: I knew the biblical principles; I had seen my share of supernatural power; I had assembled a good team; and we were prayerfully expecting God to guide us every time we hit a snag. But I was not depending on Him for something *new*. I was not hungry for *more*. Nor was I willing to lose control so that God would gain it.

I was feeding on old manna (see Exod. 16:15-21; John 6:48-50).

God told me that anyone can see His hands; servants are expected to look at their master's hands for assignments. But not everyone can see God's face, which He chooses to show only to those who crave intimacy with Him. The Lord indicated that I was confusing His anointing with His glory. The anointing may be given to anyone in order to accomplish His purposes on Earth. Even the High Priest who orchestrated Jesus' crucifixion was anointed to prophesy that "one man should die for the people" (John 11:50). God's glory comes only when we are desperately thirsty (see John 7:37-39); then we come to Jesus and drink in holy desperation.

Ed, you are not thirsty enough. Like Peter and the disciples, you know what the Scriptures say. You have figured out what needs to be done, and you are doing it the best you can. You are coming to me for guidance when you get stuck. But none of that is enough. You need to experience the fullness of the power of the Holy Spirit. You need to be driven out of the safety of the Upper Room by a mighty noise. You need to be purified by tongues of fire over your head. You need to be overcome by my Spirit to the point that you will not be afraid to lose your human dignity and lay on the ground.

Now I understood why that glass wall was there.

Later that morning I met with the team, and we corporately confessed our spiritual poverty, crying out to God for mercy. I put aside my notes for the first session. Instead, when I stood before the people I told them about the visitation, and we all lay before Him, crying out for a new day of Pentecost. Out of that first session came the clear leading that we needed to reach out to President Estrada with blessings. If I had taught instead what was on the scheduled program, good things likely would have happened. But *good* is not *the best*. Because we cried out to Him, God led us into something extraordinary—a move that has the potential to turn the presidential palace into a lighthouse of prayer!

Let us empty ourselves of every good thing we have so that God can give us the best. He alone can provide true excellence. We cannot reach our cities feeding on yesterday's manna; we need new manna every day. The books, the notes, the miracles of yesterday—all these are just old manna. We need to subscribe to the theology of more. To do so, we need to give up control and live in a constant state of awe, as did the disciples in the Early Church. They did not know what each new day would bring until they met afresh with God and He revealed it to them.

WE CAN REACH A CITY WITH HIS ANOINTING, BUT WE WILL NOT SEE THE GLORY OF GOD UNLESS WE THIRST AFTER HIM—MORE OF JESUS EVERY DAY!

We can reach a city by relying on the anointing, but we will not see the glory of God unless we thirst after Him. Begin to subscribe to the theology of more: more of Jesus every day!

God's Officer Candidate School

If you are dreaming big dreams, such as seeing your city and your nation transformed, you are positioning yourself for greater leadership. Even if you do not say it aloud, in the innermost part of your soul you are toying with the idea that you are to lead others. This may be difficult for you to verbalize because godly leaders are humble people. God has allowed you to lead in different aspects until now; but to see your city or your nation transformed, you need to move to a higher level of leadership. You need to go to God's Officer Candidate School, where the devil is the drill sergeant. Let me show you this from the Scriptures.

In Luke 22:24, we read of a dispute among the disciples as to which one of them would be regarded as the greatest. What do you picture Simon Peter doing during that dispute? Do you see him sitting quietly in a corner, reading from the book of Isaiah while praying for his immature brothers? Or do you imagine him advising the other 11 that the only spot open was number 2, since he was clearly number 1? I am sure you would agree that the latter better fits Peter's personality.

Jesus responded by first addressing all of the disciples and explaining how the kingdom of God works. He graciously promised them thrones, affirming their desire for greater leadership (v. 30). But then He switched his focus from the Twelve to the big fisherman, Peter:

> Simon, Simon, behold, Satan has demanded permission
> to sift you like wheat; but I have prayed for you, that
> your faith may not fail; and you, when once you have
> turned again, strengthen your brothers (Luke 22:31,32).

Jesus singled out Peter here, telling him that in order to lead he needed to go to officer training camp. "You will be stripped of everything but your faith, which I will preserve for you," Jesus said, in essence. "You will end up heading in the wrong direction, Peter; but when you turn around, you will provide leadership for your brothers. But not until you have graduated as an officer."

Peter's greatest asset was loyalty. As such, his greatest fear may have been to be found disloyal. And this is exactly where he ended up: He denied the Lord (see Luke 22:54-62). Peter cried bitterly but it was a cleansing cry, one that washed away all vestige of self-confidence. On that fateful night, Peter came to the end of himself and realized that he could not serve the Lord, or lead his brothers, in the natural.

He thought he was finished; but when he turned around, Peter found that the Lord had preserved his faith. It happened a few weeks later when, after having tried in vain all night to catch fish, he recognized the risen Lord calling from shore (see John 21:7). Peter jumped out of the boat and swam to meet Him and to be welcomed to enjoy the breakfast Jesus had prepared.

If we are to lead, God needs to strip us of all vestige of self-confidence, because self-confidence stands between us and total dependence on Him. To do this He allows the devil to come in like a raging flood. The very thing we fear most is what He allows to happen, and we sink to the deepest part in the ocean of our fears, so that when God's arm reaches down and pulls us up, we will know it is His power that counts and not ours.

Fear can only frighten us in the future tense. When we tell ourselves how afraid we are that such and such a thing would happen, we are most vulnerable because we are experiencing in the emotional present a situation that can only happen in the future and, as such, is beyond our control. When that which we fear comes to pass, we are finally able to do something about it besides fretting. Not even God can fix a situation that does not exist. Only when our fears come to pass is He able to deal with them.

It is only the broken vessel that the Divine Potter can remake into a new one according to His will. The power of the Resurrection requires a death first. God allows the devil to inflict such so that the Lord can resurrect us in the fullness of *His* power rather than our own.

Don't be afraid of the struggle. You will overcome in the end because the Lord will preserve your faith. Do not be afraid of being wounded; those wounds will become reminders of God's faithfulness. You may need to go through situations that to the eyes of bystanders may present you in a light that is less than satisfactory to your pride. But remember, although some people despised Jacob because he limped, only Jacob knew what it was to have wrestled with an angel and won.

If you want to see your city transformed, you need to step up in leadership. And to do so, you need to be sifted like wheat by God's drill sergeant. Welcome every trial that comes your way because it is designed to make you stronger by first taking you to the limits of yourself and then driving you into the arms of the One who has words of eternal life. When you emerge, you will be able to look the devil in the eye until he blinks. You will have been to hell and back, and you will have learned that there is no power in that dark place capable of opposing the resurrection power now operating in you.

Only Jesus Matters

When multitudes showed up unannounced, the disciples requested that Jesus dismiss them. Instead, He fed them, and He then sent the disciples ahead in the boat while He dismissed the multitude (see Matt. 14:14-22). That night, as Jesus prayed alone on the mountain, the disciples became caught in a storm at sea, "battered by the waves; for the wind was contrary" (v. 24). Then, during the darkest hour of the night, Jesus came to them, walking on the waters; but instead of being encouraged by this, the disciples "were frightened, saying, 'It is a ghost!' And they cried out for fear" (v. 26).

This is sad. Jesus walking upon the very waves that threatened them should have been a powerful and most comforting sight to the disciples. Why did they not recognize their Lord?

Because they slid down the escalator of fear. First, they were frightened—a subjective state. This means that they *felt* fear inside them. But they externalized their fear when they spoke corporately, declaring "It is a ghost!" and panic took over, making grown men cry out like scared babies. These were experienced sailors who had fished at night since childhood. So why were they suddenly in such a pitiful state? Because they took counsel from their fears.

Fear is always a poor counselor. If you hope to reach cities, you should never listen to your fears. More importantly, never hang around people who verbalize *their* fears. There is a powerful spiritual chemistry that is activated by declaring with our mouths what we have chosen to believe in our hearts, whether it is faith that saves us or fear that sinks us. When people allow their fright to become a confessed fear, panic sets in. The difference between a coward who flees and a hero who stands is minimal. The coward looks at his fright, takes counsel from it and runs. The hero is not without fear; he simply refuses the counsel of his fears and chooses to stand firm.

So how did Jesus minister to his disciples? He told them three things (v. 27):

1. "Take courage." In other words, change your attitude. Choose to face the problem, rather than run from it.
2. "It is I." This is the fact on which our faith must be based.
3. "Do not be afraid." Once our attitude has been changed and we have accepted the fact that Jesus is with us, it is very normal for us to stop being afraid.

Normally, the first thing we tell people who are afraid is that they should not be afraid. This seldom helps because fear is an emotion that paralyzes the will. Instead, we need to do what

Jesus told the disciples to do: Change your attitude. This is a decision one can make anytime, not because of psychological hyping but because Jesus is next to us. He will never leave us nor forsake us (see Heb. 13:5). He is master over the problem that is battering us.

Peter finally recognized this, and he dared to venture out of the boat and walk on water himself at the word of the Lord. How far was Peter from Jesus when he began to sink? Just a few feet, since Jesus was able to stretch out His hand and get a hold of him (see Matt. 14:31). Throughout human history, many of the greatest defeats happened within minutes of or inches from victory. Brave men quit and went down in defeat when they could have been crowned with victory had they persisted just a little bit longer.

When the British surrendered Singapore during World War II, the Japanese commander scolded his fallen foes, telling them that if they had fought only a few more hours, *he* would have been the one surrendering. He was fast running out of ammunition and supplies; the British had surrendered with plenty of both.

As discussed in the opening chapter, we are often much closer to victory than the enemy wants us to know. Peter's success and failure on the water illustrates this. With minimal faith he said to Jesus, "Lord, if it is You, command me to come to You on the water" (v. 28). He was not taking any risks. Peter asked the Lord to *make* him do it. And he was doing well until he focused on the wind.

It is important to note that what brought Peter down was not the waves that were buffeting the boat but the wind (see Matt. 14:30). This is important for two reasons. As an experienced fisherman, Peter was in his element. He knew the characteristics of water and how to deal with waves. But the wind was something else. Peter succumbed because of his inability to handle something that was beyond his normal area of expertise.

This is often true of Christians today. This is why we need to learn to walk by faith in new areas. Yesterday's manna is no good for today. God will allow the devil to push us out of our areas of natural abilities so that through a failure in the natural, we will learn to rely on God in the supernatural.

The second reason Peter started to sink had to do with Peter's objective. He was almost to Jesus when he began to sink. Why would he lose it so close to the Lord? Because Peter's ultimate goal was not to be near Jesus but to make it to shore. We know this because the Bible says "the wind was contrary" (v. 24), which means the wind was blowing away from the shore, the direction sailors head when caught in a storm. Peter lost it when he *saw* the wind (see v. 30). One cannot see the wind without a visible frame of reference, which for Peter had to be the shoreline. Peter sank because his objective was to make it to shore, not to be with Jesus.

Reaching a city for Christ is important, but it pales in comparison to drawing near to Jesus. Our objective cannot be to reach a city; it must be intimacy with Jesus. If we are going to walk on water, it cannot be to display our faith but to draw closer to Him. Whether we reach a city or not, our driving passion has to be intimacy with the Lord.

If we draw near to Jesus, we will then bring Him into the boat, the wind will stop, and those who were paralyzed by fear will declare, "You are certainly God's Son!" (v. 33)—a definite improvement from "He is a ghost!" Better yet, the boat will not turn back to the shore from where we sailed but, instead, it will cross over to Gennesaret, the place we almost turned our backs on when the storm hit. And the people there will touch Jesus and as many as touch Him will be cured (see vv. 34-36).

Can you imagine how differently things would have turned out if the disciples, with their proven dislike of crowds, would have made it to Gennesaret ahead of Jesus? They may have dismissed the people or allowed only a few to see Jesus. Instead, because of the storm, they learned a valuable lesson and arrived in Gennesaret to see people and a region transformed.

This is the beauty of trials. They force us to exchange our good things for His excellence. They teach us how to face the devil in God's power by rendering our power useless. We soon learn that we can only overcome the adversary in the power of the resurrection made real by the faith that Jesus preserved for us. And when everything is said and done, we know that the only thing that counts is Jesus. It is not what we do for Him. It is Him. Only Him.

When we finally stand before the judgment seat of Christ, each of us will stand alone. No one else will take our place when our turn comes to face the Lord. No other Christians, no other pastors, no other city reachers—just Christ and me. It is my desire, and I pray it becomes my ambition also, that on that day I will be drawn to Him by the consuming desire to embrace the One who embraced me when I was lost; that this desire would be so rooted in me that when He goes down the list of things for which He is pleased with me, I will be as perplexed as the righteous described in Matthew 25:37-40 who did so much for Jesus without realizing it.

How can a person give water to the thirsty, feed the hungry and visit prisoners, and not realize that he or she is doing these things to Jesus? Because when we are so focused on Him and Him alone, the doing does not matter. It is being with Him that counts, and when we are with Him, passionately in love with Him, we always take care of those He came to seek and save.

If we are so focused on Jesus and Him alone, the storm around us will die down, and multitudes will confess that He is certainly God's Son. They will do it not because of our expertise, but because of our dependence on Him.

Let us make Jesus our only consuming passion. Then, and only then, will we be ready to see our cities transformed.

Note
1. Mike Richardson, a former missionary to Argentina with Harvest Evangelism, is the executive pastor of Hosanna Christian Fellowship in Phoenix, Arizona.

Additional Works by Ed Silvoso

THAT NONE SHOULD PERISH VIDEO SEMINAR
This breakthrough video series is the live version of Ed Silvoso's best-selling book, *That None Should Perish*. Each of the sixteen lessons are broken into 35 minute segments, which makes it perfect for Bible studies, Sunday School classes, or pastors prayer groups. Includes reproducible syllabus. (Four 2-hour videotapes)

LIGHT THE NATION ONE HOUSE AT A TIME Starter Kit
This starter kit by Ed Silvoso includes a 7-minute motivational video, 30-minute how-to audio cassette on Lighthouses of Prayer and a Lighthouse Guidebook. This is an excellent motivational and training tool for both individuals and groups. (Video tape, audio tape, guidebook)

VICTORY AT HOME!
This four tape audio series is a timely message that will help parents prepare their children for a successful marriage, as well as evaluate the condition of their own marriage relationship. Singles will also find this series encouraging as they trust God for their life partner. (Four 60-minute audio tapes)

BECOMING AN OVERCOMER
This two tape series will help you to not only pull down the strongholds that have kept you from living a victorious Christian life, but will also allow you to see how God can turn the worst tragedy in your life into a trophy of His love when grace is applied to those who have hurt you. Two life-changing topics! (Two 60-minute audio tapes)

Acquire these and other titles through Harvest Evangelism's on-line bookstore at www.harvestevan.org, or by contacting them at:

Harvest Evangelism, Inc.
P.O. Box 20310 • San Jose, CA 95160-0310
Tel (800)835-7979 • (408)350-1669 • Fax (408)927-9830

Experience Prayer Evangelism first-hand with Ed Silvoso by participating in one of Harvest Evangelism's Argentina training trips (Summer and Fall).
Call (408)927-9052 today.